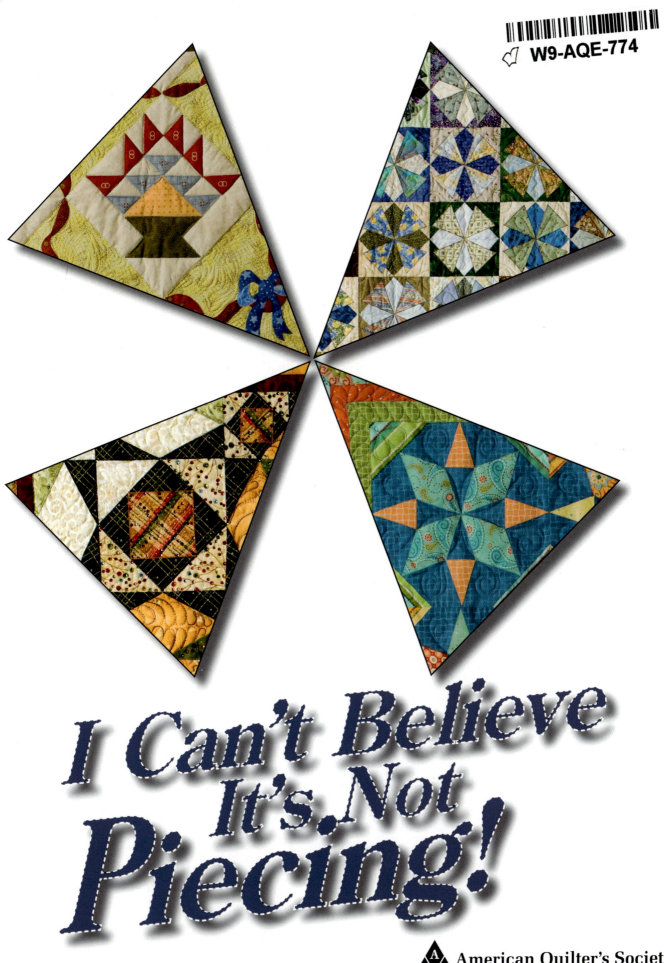

I Can't Believe It's Not Piecing!

American Quilter's Society

P. O. Box 3290 • Paducah, KY 42002-3290
www.AmericanQuilter.com

DEDICATION

Lovingly dedicated to our dear mother,
Ava Atwood Winterton

ACKNOWLEDGMENTS

First of all, we would like to thank our husbands, Richard Seely and Lynn Stewart, who have been so supportive and so patient. They don't always understand this "quilt thing" but they love us and that is what's more important. We would like to thank all of our children and grandchildren who think it's awesome that they have a mom and a grandma who make quilts to keep them warm and cozy, and can actually write a book!

A big "thank you" to our editor, Andi Reynolds, for believing in us right from the start and helping us turn our dream into a reality. Also, thanks to our graphic designer, Barry Buchanan, and to Charles R. Lynch for the great photography.

A special thanks to Joyce's daughter, Susan Watkins, for making CORAL TIDES and PINWHEELS WITH PIZZAZZ. All of the other quilts were made by the two of us. All of the quilts were machine quilted by Ann.

We would also like to acknowledge quiltmakers everywhere. We believe that a quiltmaker is more than just someone who makes quilts. A quiltmaker loves geometric shapes, the soft curves of floral appliqué, the interplay of color, freshly pressed fabric, and the feel of quilting stitches. Quiltmaker is a term of endearment!

Located in Paducah, Kentucky, the American Quilter's Society (AQS) is dedicated to promoting the accomplishments of today's quilters. Through its publications and events, AQS strives to honor today's quiltmakers and their work and to inspire future creativity and innovation in quiltmaking.

Text © 2010, Authors, Ann Seely and Joyce Stewart.

Artwork © 2010, American Quilter's Society

Executive Book Editor: Andi Milam Reynolds
Graphic Design: Barry Buchanan
Cover Design: Michael Buckingham
Photography: Charles R. Lynch

Additional copies of this book may be ordered from the American Quilter's Society, PO Box 3290, Paducah, KY 42002-3290, or online at www.AmericanQuilter.com.

Library of Congress Cataloging-in-Publication Data

Seely, Ann.
  I can't believe it's not piecing! / by Ann Seely and Joyce Stewart.
    p. cm.
  ISBN 978-1-57432-669-7
  1. Machine appliqué--Patterns. I. Stewart, Joyce, 1939- II. Title.
  TT779.S365 2010
  746.44'5--dc22
                                           2010020879

Proudly printed and bound in the United States of America

CONTENTS

INTRODUCTION

Somewhere back in the far reaches of history a woman cut small squares of fabric and stitched them together, piece by piece. Since that day piecing has been the backbone of quiltmaking.

There are literally hundreds of pieced block designs: some are simple and others have more tiny squares and triangles than anyone would care to count.

Early piecing and appliqué (the layering of one fabric on top of another) were done by hand. With the availability of the sewing machine, piecing gained popularity because it was much faster to piece the patches together. Appliqué remained handwork because sewing machines could not replicate the desired effect.

Piecing is still popular today, but many quilters shy away from some pieced designs because they are much too complicated to fit today's fast-paced lifestyle. Some quilters don't like to sew blocks with set-in seams. Curved piecing is especially frustrating because, typically, it is difficult to keep the block perfectly flat.

Our solution to the problem of complicated piecing is to take advantage of the fact that today's sewing machines can do beautiful appliqué in a fraction of the time it takes to piece the same design.

By combining templates for accuracy and simple, straight-seam piecing with machine appliqué, we can cut down on the bulk of multiple seams or the bulge of curved seams and still maintain the look of precision piecing that we love.

Once you try this combination piecing/machine appliqué technique, you will look forward to "seamlessly" piecing even the most complex block. The design possibilities are endless. People will admire your quilts and say, "I can't believe it's not piecing!"

Fabric

Fabrics inspire us! The palette of colors and range of printed designs seem to get more beautiful every year as manufacturers try to satisfy quilters' appetites.

As you may have discovered, not all 100 percent cotton fabric is the same quality. Manufacturers make different quality grades of base fabric so it can be sold at different prices. Usually the feel or the "hand" of the fabric will identify the quality of the fabric. Scrunch it in your hand; if it wrinkles easily or stays wrinkled after smoothing, it is not desirable for your quilt. Lower quality fabric will also have a lower thread count. The best quality fabric will be easier to sew, will press nicely, and will look and feel better.

We recommend washing your fabric in mild detergent and steam pressing the fabric before using. Washing removes any excess color or sizing and gives good quality fabric an even softer feel.

We also recommend removing the selvage edges before sewing. If left in a quilt, the edge will shrink at a different rate than the rest of the yardage. It should be removed prior to cutting the fabric to press the yardage without the edges puckering. It is especially important to cut or tear off the selvage edges when piecing the backing together.

Quilts can become heirlooms that last for generations. The best way you can ensure—from the very beginning—that your quilt will be the best it can be is to always purchase 100 percent cotton fabric of the highest quality. We encourage you to support your local fabric stores and quilt shops, as they work hard to have the very best, highest quality, and newest quilting fabrics available for your use.

Thread

Thread is the second most important element of your quilt, yet many quiltmakers don't give the thread much thought. After all, just about any thread will hold the pieces together and it doesn't show, right? So what is all the fuss about thread?

Just as fabric differs in quality, so does thread. Look closely at your thread. Pull out a single strand and hold it to the light. Does it appear a bit furry? Does the thickness vary even a teeny bit? Do you seem to have trouble with the tension in your sewing machine? Does your thread break when you are sewing with it? These are signs of poor quality thread. For piecing, we recommend Superior MasterPiece™ thread 50 wt./2-ply. It is very strong and is virtually lint-free.

Our "I can't believe it's not piecing" technique, something we also call "seamless piecing," is really machine appliqué, so the thread you choose will show. For machine appliqué, we recommend a high quality 100 percent cotton 40 wt. thread, but a good quality polyester thread can give satisfactory results. We like Gutermann® or Mettler® cotton or polyester 40 wt. For an almost invisible look, match the color of thread to the appliqué fabric as closely as possible. The best way to do this is to lay a single strand of thread on top of your fabric. You may be surprised at how different the color looks off of the spool.

The correct thread in your bobbin is crucial, too. We have found that using a thinner thread in the bobbin and tightening the bobbin tension slightly will help keep the bobbin thread from showing through on the top of the appliqué. We like 60 wt. Superior Bottom Line™ lint-free polyester. Wind a neutral gray thread in the bobbin and you can use it with any top thread color except white, which calls for white in the bobbin

Decorative threads are an option, also. There are many kinds of decorative threads, each with its own specific qualities. Sometimes a decorative thread will add another dimension to your work.

Always follow the manufacturers' recommendations for use, including what size needle works best. When using variegated quilting thread, we recommend Superior King Tut™ quilting thread .

Needles

A small needle makes a small stitch. A sharp point sewing machine needle size 80/12 is fine for sewing seams, but for stitching the appliqué shapes in this book we recommend using a 60/8 sharp point needle. A 70/10 size needle is also acceptable. Thicker thread and a larger needle are required if you use wool pieces for the appliqué or wool thread for stitching the appliqués. Replace your machine needles often. A dull or bent needle can ruin your work.

Never, never, never give up.
- Winston Churchill
Never, never, never sew over pins.
- Anonymous Quilter

Sewing Machine Tips

Use an open-toe embroidery foot so you can see exactly where you are stitching as you machine appliqué.

A small blanket stitch gives the nicest "seamless piecing" look. It should have a forward stitch of about ⅛" or less and an inner bite of about ⅛" or less. A small, narrow zigzag also works well.

Fusible Web

Seamless piecing/machine appliqué requires the use of a lightweight fusible web such as HeatnBond® Lite. Always follow the manufacturer's instructions for using any fusible-web product.

Templates

The key to success for the precision-piecing look is the accuracy of the templates. Templates are used over and over and must stand up to the job. Plastic template material is sold at most quilt shops and works great. It is easy to use and comes in plain sheets or printed with a graph-paper grid. Heavier paper such as cardstock also works well, but doesn't hold up as long as plastic. Paper templates will have to be replaced when they begin to show wear.

Seams

All the seams in our patterns are ¼" seams. For the most accurate ¼" seams, we suggest using a quarter-inch foot while piecing. If one is not available for your sewing machine, carefully measure one-quarter inch from the needle and mark the place with masking tape.

Where appliqué is to be stitched over the seams, press the seams open so that the appliqué will lie flat. Otherwise, press seams toward the darker fabric.

Before You Begin

Sample Block

Making a sample block is optional, but it is always a good idea. You can use odds and ends of fabric from your stash. Making a sample block takes a little time at first but will save fabric, time, and frustration over the long term. Once you've made a sample block, you can make any corrections to your templates or pattern before tracing all of the templates onto the fusible web.

Backing

Backing fabric should be the same quality 100 percent cotton fabric as used on the quilt top. The backing should be several inches wider and longer than the quilt top, as extra width and length are desirable when quilting, whether by hand or machine.

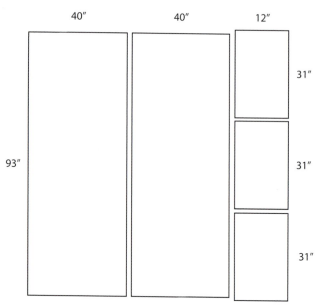

This is one example of how to cut and piece fabric to make a backing. Any method of piecing strips or pieces of fabric together that results in a backing wide enough and long enough will do.

MACHINE APPLIQUÉ

Seamless piecing may seem like an oxymoron, but it really means a new way of looking at pieced blocks and recreating them with template-based machine appliqué. It is fun to do and the results are terrific! The only actual piecing required is very simple, straight-line piecing, easy enough for even the most novice quilter.

You won't need any new tools or a fancy sewing machine; a simple blanket stitch or tiny zigzag will do the job. As with any new method, it may require a bit of practice, but in a short amount of time you will be precision sewing like a pro.

Before beginning any project read through the instructions. Doing this will familiarize you with the method and any necessary supplies or special techniques. The basic steps are simple, but it is important that you follow each of them carefully.

It is wise to make one sample block before cutting all of the fabric for all of the blocks, in case you need to adjust the pattern or any templates.

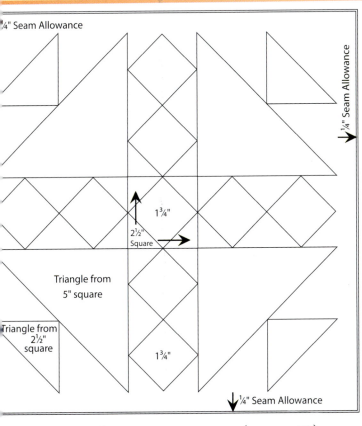

¼" Seam Allowance

¼" Seam Allowance

1¾"

2½"
Square

Triangle from
5" square

Triangle from
2½"
square

1¾"

1¾"

¼" Seam Allowance

This example is the Bits & Pieces pattern (see page 22).

Step One: Prepare the Paper Pattern

If necessary, enlarge the pattern to the correct (finished block) size. Darken the lines on the block with a medium tip black marker so that the lines can be easily seen through fabric. Use a light source such as a light box or window, and a ruler so that the lines are nice and straight.

Step Two: Prepare the Background

> *Note* Some block backgrounds will be a single piece of fabric and some may require simple piecing.

Make sure the paper pattern of the block includes the seam allowance so that it will line up perfectly along the outside edges of the block. Tape the paper pattern to a light box or to a window. Place the fabric over the pattern and tape it down so it doesn't slip.

Trace the lines on the right side of the fabric with a removable marker that shows up well on each particular fabric, such as a water-soluble marker or a chalk marker. These lines will be the reference marks when pressing the appliqué shapes onto the fabric. Be extremely accurate. Mark each of the blocks exactly the same.

Step Three: Make the Templates

Determine the shapes needed for the project, and then make the templates. Template plastic purchased from a quilt shop is easy to use and very durable. Use a ruler to make straight lines and cut out the templates as accurately as possible.

Templates can also be made from medium-weight paper such as cardstock or an old manila folder. First make three or four paper copies of the actual size block. Save one as a master copy.

From the other copies, rough cut the shapes needed and adhere them to the cardstock with rubber cement or a good quality glue stick. Label your templates. Then, cut them out as precisely as possible, cutting the pencil/pen edge off, and voila!—a perfect template. The edges of the paper templates will wear down with use and the template will need to be replaced. Only one template per shape is needed.

Step Four: Make Fusible-Web Shapes

Trace around the templates onto the fusible web. Some shapes, such as squares and rectangles, will not require a template, but can be drawn directly onto the fusible web using a pencil and a plastic ruler. Try to make the best use of the fusible web so there is very little waste.

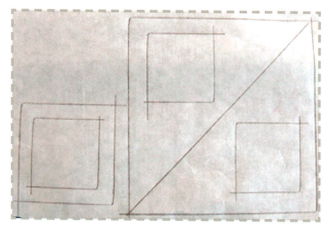

Small shapes can be traced inside the larger shapes because the fusible web will be cut away inside the shape. Remember to leave at least ¼" between pattern pieces so that they can be cut apart.

It is easy to keep track of the fusible-web shapes if you label them. To label the shapes, simply write a number/letter just inside the line of the shape, so that the labeling will not be cut off when cutting away the inside of the shapes.

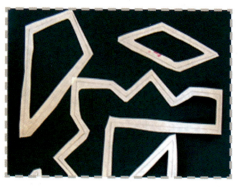

Cut the fusible-web pattern pieces apart, but do not cut them on the exact lines yet. The most important thing to remember is to cut away the inside of the fusible web leaving a scant ¼" all around. Otherwise, the block will be stiff, making the whole quilt stiff and uncomfortable. Save the cut-away pieces of fusible web to use for small appliqués.

Step Five: Press the Fusible Web to the Fabric and Cut Out Templates or Shapes

Press the fusible web to the wrong side of the chosen fabrics and cut them apart, but do not cut out on the lines yet. Cut the pieces to the exact size only when ready to press them into place to prevent fraying. You can also cut down on fraying by placing the fusible-web pieces on the bias of the fabric.

Cut long straight lines with a rotary cutter and a plastic ruler. When cutting out the fusible-web pieces, cut off the pencil line as even this small amount may make the piece a little too large.

When cutting the centers out of fusible-web squares/rectangles which have been drawn through on the diagonal to create triangles, cut out the inside of each triangle separately. Do not cut the square/rectangle into triangles until after the square has been pressed to the fabric.

Step Six: Press the Appliqué Shapes to the Block

Cut out the fusible-web shapes to the exact size. Remove the paper backing of the fusible web and press the appliqué shapes to the block. Press the pieces in the order given per project.

If possible, press all of the pieces that use the same color of thread onto the block at the same time; this will cut down on repeatedly changing the thread color. For example, press all the red squares in each block and stitch them down before pressing and stitching any of the other pieces. Do this for each thread color.

Step Seven: Stitch the Appliqué Shapes

Stitch the appliqué shapes in place. Begin and end the stitches where they will show the least. After ending off, leave a long tail of thread and pull the threads to the back.

Hint A self-threading needle makes quick work of pulling the threads to the back. Tie the threads to secure them. Trim the threads. From the front, it should not be obvious where the stitching started and ended.

If another piece of appliqué will cover where the stitching starts and stops, it is not necessary to tie off the threads; just trim the threads close on both the front and the back of the block.

Take short stitches—⅛" or less. The stitches should bite into the fabric ⅛" or less, unless larger stitches are desired for decorative purposes.

If hand quilting, you may trim the fabric away from behind the appliqué, leaving at least ⅜" inside the edges so as not to weaken the appliqué. This will eliminate bulk and make it easier to quilt. Trimming is optional if the quilt will be quilted by machine.

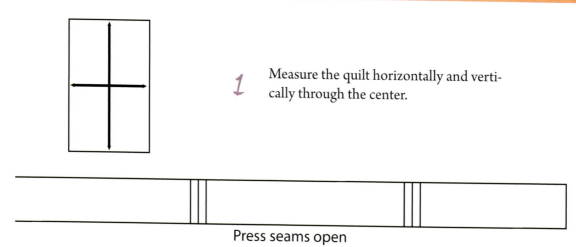

1 Measure the quilt horizontally and vertically through the center.

Press seams open

2 Cut borders crosswise or on the straight grain of fabric. To determine how long to cut the borders to have plenty of fabric for mitering, measure the width of the border strip and double this amount. Add this measurement to the total width/length of the quilt top. For instance, if the quilt top measures 50" wide/long and the border strip is 5" wide, the border strip must be at least 50"+5"+5" or 60" wide/long. Add two or three inches for "insurance." This will be trimmed off but makes for easier handling.

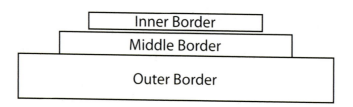

3 Multiple fabrics can be sewn together and treated as a single unit. Because the border strip is cut on the diagonal at each corner, the inner border measurement will be less than the outer border measurement. This means that the borders can be cut at different lengths to save fabric. Cut the border strips the lengths specified in the pattern, match the centers, pin and sew them together in "stair-step" fashion.

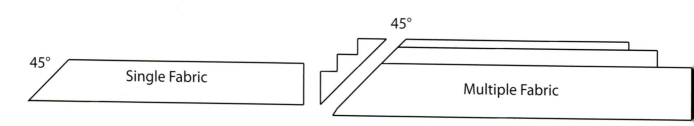

4 Using a rotary cutter and plastic ruler, cut one end of the border strip at a 45-degree angle.

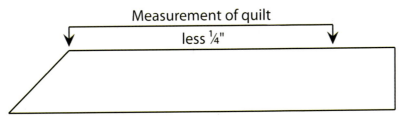

Measurement of quilt

less ¼"

5   Measure along the inner edge and mark the point that equals the width of the quilt *minus ¼"*.

45°   45°

6   Using this mark as a reference, cut the border strip at a 45-degree angle in the opposite direction from the first cut.

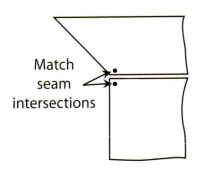

Match seam intersections

7   Mark ¼" seam intersections on the wrong sides of all corners of the quilt and inside edges of the borders. Matching ¼" seam intersections, pin and sew the borders to the quilt, starting and stopping at the ¼" marks.

8   Pin and sew all four mitered corners, beginning at the outside edge of the corner and sewing towards the quilt. Backstitch.

Note   If the border strips need to be pieced, trim off any selvage edges and pin the strips right sides together. Sew the strips together with a ¼" seam and press the seam open. Make the border strips the required lengths specified in the pattern.

BINDING

These instructions are for 3" double-fold binding.

To prepare the quilt for binding, trim the raw edges of the quilt straight using a rotary cutter and a plastic ruler. Pin and baste the top, batting, and backing layers together close to the edge to keep the layers from shifting, and to help flatten the quilt edge for a nicer binding result.

To figure how much binding you will need, measure around the circumference of the quilt and add 18" for seaming and overlap. If you need a total of 208" of binding, divide 208" by 40 (width of fabric) to determine the number of strips you will need. In this case you would need 6 strips. Cut 3" strips on the crosswise or the straight grain of the fabric.

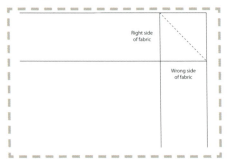

1 To piece the binding strips together, turn one of the strips a quarter-turn and place it on top of the next strip, right sides together. Mark and sew a diagonal seam as shown. Trim, leaving a ¼" seam allowance. Press the seam open. Trim the tails. Repeat as needed, making the binding at least 12" longer than the perimeter of the quilt.

Fold the binding in half lengthwise, wrong sides together. Press, keeping the raw edges lined up.

Using an even-feed foot and a long stitch length, baste the raw edges of the binding strip together close to the raw edge. If an even-feed foot is not available, pin the raw edges of the binding strip together every few inches to keep the raw edges from shifting, then baste the raw edges together.

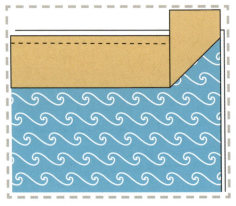

2 Leave a "tail" of binding about 8" long. Sew the binding to the right side of the quilt, through all of the layers, keeping all the basted edges aligned. Sew ⅜" from the outer edge. Stop sewing ⅜" from the corner of the quilt. Backstitch and remove the quilt from the machine. Fold the binding strip up at a 45-degree angle.

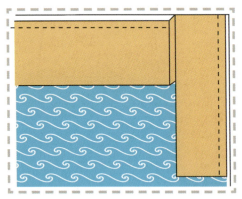

3 Fold the strip down making a fold at the upper edge. The fold should line up straight with the top edge of the quilt. Begin sewing at the upper edge using a ⅜" seam. Continue sewing around the quilt, mitering all four corners.

Stop sewing approximately 12" from where the stitching began. Remove the quilt from the machine.

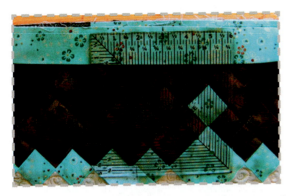

4 Find the center of the "unsewn" space and cut off one of the "tails" 1½" past this line. Cut the "tail" straight using a rotary cutter and plastic ruler. Overlap the "tails" and make a mark at the 3" line as shown. Cut the second tail at the 3" mark. The binding strips should overlap each other by exactly 3 inches.

Remove the basting stitches from the binding strips, where the strip has not yet been sewn.

6 Baste the raw edges of the binding together, close to the edge. Pin and sew the binding to the quilt. Turn the binding to the back of the quilt and hand sew it in place.

Note Since all battings are different thicknesses, the seam width may have to be adjusted, i.e., a bit narrower to allow for thicker batting, or a bit wider for extra thin batting. When the binding is finished and turned to the back, the binding should line up with the stitching line on the back of the quilt.

5 Turn one binding strip a quarter turn and place against the other binding strip, right sides together. Mark and sew a diagonal seam. Press the seam open.

Option Sew the binding to the back of the quilt instead of to the front of the quilt. Fold the binding to the front and hand or machine sew the binding in place. Use a decorative stitch if desired.

Apple Pickin' Time

64" x 64". Made by Joyce Stewart; quilted by Ann Seely.

Apple pickin' time in the fall meant that many of our friends and their parents would gather to harvest apples from the farm our church owned. Mostly the kids just chased each other around the trees while the grown-ups picked. The apples were distributed to those in need and each family that helped received a bushel of red, juicy apples to take home.

Materials

- ⅜ yard each of 13 different medium prints (triangles for blocks)
- 2¼ yards dark red (accent squares and triangles and binding)
- 2 yards tan stripe (border)
- 4¼ yards backing
- 2 yards fusible web
- 72" x 72" square batting
- Matching thread for appliqué
- 1 sheet 8½" x 11" template plastic

Templates

Refer to *Step Three: Make the Templates* under **Machine Appliqué** on page 7 and make templates that are 2" square and 2⅞" square.

Cutting

Cut and piece the border strips together following the **Mitered Borders** instructions on page 10.

Fabric

Medium Prints

2 squares 12" from each print for a total of 26 squares

Cut these squares in half diagonally, and then diagonally again going in the opposite direction, making 4 triangles from each square for a total of 104 triangles. The quilt requires 100 triangles. Use the extras to juggle color placement.

Tan Stripe

4 strips 8½" x the length of the fabric (borders)

Dark Red

1 strip 3" x 268" (binding). Cut and piece the strips together following the **Binding** instructions on page 12.

Fusible Web

Refer to *Step Four: Make Fusible-Web Shapes* under **Machine Appliqué** on page 8 for valuable tips. When cutting the centers out of the fusible-web squares which have been drawn through on the diagonal, cut out the inside of each triangle separately. Do not cut the square into triangles until after the square has been pressed to the fabric.

25 squares 2" x 2" (press to dark red)
36 squares 2⅞" x 2⅞" (press to dark red)
150 squares 2" x 2" drawn through on the diagonal, making 2 small triangles from each square for a total of 300 small triangles (press to dark red)

Apple Pickin' Time

The Blocks (10" x 10" finished)

1 Lay out the medium print triangles, keeping two triangles using the same fabric together to make a square on point. Fill in the outside edges with additional triangles. Keep these on the design wall so that you can return them to their correct position as you work, keeping the design together.

3 Trim the block to 10½" square.

2 Sew 4 of the medium print triangles together as shown, using 4 different fabrics. Press the seams open to eliminate bulk.

4 Each time a block is finished, make sure that the fabrics in the adjoining blocks match so each fabric looks like a square on point.

5 The finished block should measure 10" square. Make sure the 2" square and the triangles made from the 2" squares match the pattern. Tape the pattern to a light source. Place a fabric block with the right-side up directly over the pattern, tape it down, and trace the pattern onto the block using a water-soluble marker or a white chalk pencil.

7 Using a ruler, draw lines from each mark to the next mark, so that the triangle pieces will have a straight guideline.

6 If the blocks are busy or dark, mark the pattern in a different manner. Fold the paper pattern in half diagonally and place the pattern along the diagonal of the block. With a water-soluble marker or a chalk pencil, mark each place on the fabric where the squares and triangles begin and end. Mark both diagonals of the block.

8 Each block uses 1 dark red 2" square and 12 of the dark red triangles. Place these pieces on the block, lining up the pieces along the seams of the fabric and the drawn lines, using care to ensure accuracy. Press the center square on first, matching the corners to the seam lines. Place a set of three triangles, then a second set, etc., until all of the pieces are pressed in place.

Machine appliqué around the edges of the square and the triangles, beginning and ending at one of the corners of the square.

Make a total of 25 blocks, setting them 5 blocks across and 5 blocks down. Keep the blocks in order, replacing each block as soon as the stitching is finished. This will keep them in the correct position for sewing the blocks together.

Apple Pickin' Time

Assembly

9 Sew rows 1 and 2 together and place a dark red 2⅞" square at each place where 4 of the blocks meet, matching the corners of the square with the seam lines. Press and stitch. Cut out the center part behind each dark red 2⅞" square to remove the bulk. In the same manner, sew row 3 and row 4 together. Sew row 5 to rows 3 and 4. Sew the two sections together.

The Border

Use the 4 tan stripe strips to create the borders, referring to **Mitered Borders** on page 10 for instructions on how to make and add the mitered border to the quilt top.

Accent Blocks and Triangles

10 Place the remaining 20 dark red 2⅞" squares around the border and corners, lining up the corners of the squares with the seam lines between the blocks and the seam lines of the border. Press and stitch in place. Cut away the bulk.

Quilting and Finishing

Make a backing 72" x 72." Layer the backing, batting and quilt top. Quilt as desired. Trim and square the sandwich. Refer to **Binding** on page 12 to make and apply a 3" double-fold binding. Spritz, rinse or wash the quilt to remove any visible water-soluble markings

Enlarge 30% to 8" x 8". Add 1" seam allowance around the edges for 10½" square.

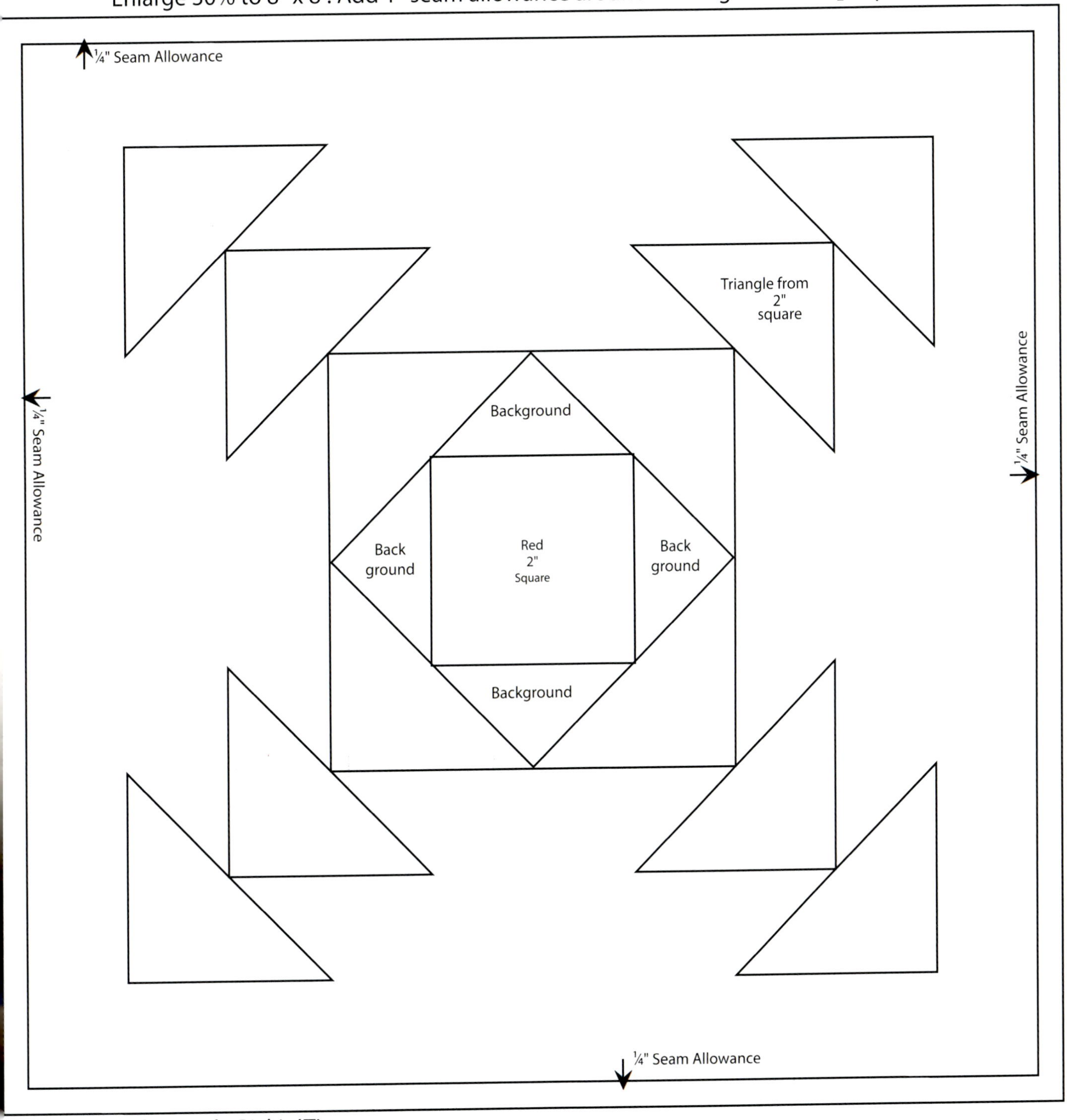

¼" Seam Allowance

¼" Seam Allowance

¼" Seam Allowance

Triangle from
2"
square

Background

Back
ground

Red
2"
Square

Back
ground

Background

¼" Seam Allowance

Template for Apple Pickin' Time.

Bits & Pieces

82" x 95". Made by Joyce Stewart; quilted by Ann Seely.

Dad was a machinist by trade so he understood precise measurements. He also loved woodworking and taught us the principle of "measure twice, cut once." He understood buying fabric, cutting it up and sewing it back together because that is what he did with lumber. He was thrifty and proud that we used all our little bits and pieces.

Materials

For each fabric listed use 30 pieces of scraps sized as follows for the blocks (a total of 150 pieces). You will have a little left over from each scrap:

14" x 14" light (background)
6" x 15" floral (large triangles and square)
4" x 6" dark (squares)
4" x 4" medium light (squares)
3" x 6" medium (small triangles)
2 yards dark green (squares, triangles, inner border, binding)
2¼ yards medium gold (outer border)
5¾ yards backing
7 yards fusible web
Queen-size quilt batt
Variegated or matching threads for appliqué, as desired
1 sheet 8½" x 11" template plastic

Templates

Refer to *Step Three: Make the Templates* under **Machine Appliqué** on page 7 and make templates that are 1¾" square, 2½" square, 2⅞" square, 3¼" square, 3⅝" square, and 5" square.

Cutting

Fabric

Cut and piece the border strips together following the **Mitered Borders** instructions on page 10.

Medium Gold

2 strips 7½" x 88" (top and bottom outer borders)
2 strips 7½" x 98" (side outer borders)

Dark Green

2 strips 2" x 76" (top and bottom inner borders)
2 strips 2" x 88" (side inner borders)

1 strip 3" x 372" (binding). Cut and piece 10 strips together following the **Binding** instructions on page 12.

Fusible Web

Refer to *Step 4: Make Fusible-Web Shapes* under **Machine Appliqué** on page 8 for valuable tips. When cutting the centers out of the fusible-web squares which have been drawn through on the diagonal, cut out the inside of each triangle separately. Do not cut the square into triangles until after the square has been pressed to the fabric.

These pieces are for the entire quilt:

20 squares 3¼" (press to dark green)
9 squares 3⅝" – drawn through on the diagonal, making 2 triangles from each square for a total of 18 triangles (press to dark green)
2 squares 2⅞" – drawn through on the diagonal, making 2 triangles from each square for a total of 4 corner triangles (press to dark green)

These pieces are for one block:

1 square 2½" (press to one of the floral scraps)
2 squares 5" – drawn through on the diagonal, making 2 triangles from each square for a total of 4 triangles (press to the same floral as the 2½" square)
5 squares 1¾" (press to one of the dark scraps)
4 squares 1¾" (press to one of the medium-light scraps)
2 squares 2½" – drawn through on the diagonal, making 2 triangles from each square for a total of 4 triangles (press to one of the medium scraps)

Repeat, making enough for 30 blocks.

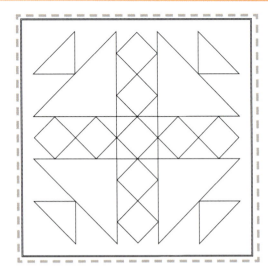

1 Use the Bits & Pieces pattern on page 7. Enlarge it 70% or until it measures 14" x 14". The blocks finish at 13½" x 13½". Tape the pattern to a light source. Place one of the 14" light background squares with the right-side up directly over the pattern, tape it down, and trace the pattern onto the square using a water-soluble marker. Use a ruler as these lines need to be accurate. Repeat for all 30 blocks.

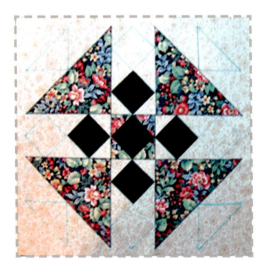

2 Place a 2½" floral square in the center of the block. Press. Place the matching floral triangles. Press. Machine appliqué around all 5 pieces in a continuous line, beginning and ending at one of the corners of the floral square. Place 5 dark 1¾" squares. Press and stitch around these squares, beginning and ending at one of the corners of the dark square in the center.

3 Place 4 medium-light 1¾" squares. Press and stitch. Place 4 triangles made from the medium 2½" squares. Press and stitch. Make a total of 30 blocks.

The Blocks (13½" x 13½" finished)

Assembly

Place the blocks on a wall or floor and decide on an arrangement, setting them 5 blocks across and 6 blocks down. Pin a number to each block to keep track of where it goes in the quilt.

4 Sew rows 1 and 2 together. Add dark green 3¼" squares where the blocks meet, using the seams of the blocks as placement guides. Add dark green triangles made from the 3⅝" squares along the outside edges, using the seams of the blocks and the edges of the quilt top as guides. Add dark green triangles made from the 2⅞" squares on the corners, using the edges of the quilt as guides. Press and stitch. Do not stitch the triangles along the outside edges of the quilt as these edges will become part of the seam. Sew rows 3 and 4 together. Sew rows 5 and 6 together. Sew all 3 sets of rows together. Add additional dark green squares and triangles.

The Borders

Use the medium-gold and dark-green strips to create the borders, referring to **Mitered Borders** on page 10 for instructions on how to make and add the mitered border to the quilt top.

Quilting and Finishing

Make a backing 90" x 103". Layer the backing, batting and quilt top. Quilt as desired. Trim and square the sandwich. Refer to **Binding** on page 12 to make and apply a 3" double-fold binding. Spritz, rinse or wash the quilt to remove any visible water-soluble markings.

Double Take

50" x 80". Made by Joyce Stewart; quilted by Ann Seely.

When Mom and Dad honeymooned in Yellowstone National Park, camping under the stars was the norm and bears were a common sight. One night Mom felt a soft, wet kiss and thought it was Dad, but when she opened her eyes, she did a double take. It was a big brown bear! Her scream ing sent the bear running and they spent the rest of the tr sleeping on the flat-top roof of their 1935 Nash.

Materials

1½ yards medium-dark blue (inner border, cornerstones, binding)

1½ yards small white print #1 (background)

1½ yards small white print #2 (background)

¼ yard each of at least 14 assorted medium prints (Bear Paws and sashings; Joyce used 20 prints in DOUBLE TAKE.)

1¼ yards blue floral print (outer border)

3½ yards backing

4 yards fusible web

Twin-size quilt batt

Variegated threads for appliqué

1 sheet 8½" x 11" template plastic

Assorted Medium Prints

45 strips 1¾" x 9¼" strips (sashings; use each fabric 3 or 4 times)

Blue Floral

2 strips 4½" x 56" (top and bottom outer borders)

2 strips 4½" x 86" (top and bottom outer borders)

Fusible Web

Refer to *Step Four: Make Fusible-Web Shapes* under **Machine Appliqué** on page 8 for valuable tips.

112 Template A (press to assorted medium prints; 2 sets of 4 from each fabric)

28 1¼" squares (press to assorted medium prints; 2 from each fabric)

Templates

Refer to *Step Three: Make the Templates* under **Machine Appliqué** on page 7 and make Template A and a 1¼" square template.

Cutting

Cut and piece the border strips together following the **Mitered Borders** instructions on page 10.

Fabric

Medium-dark Blue

18 squares 1¾" x 1¾" (cornerstones)

2 strips 2" x 52" (top and bottom inside borders)

2 strips 2" x 82" (side inside borders)

1 strip 3" x 278" (binding). Cut and piece the strips together following the **Binding** instructions, page 12.

Small White Print #1

14 squares 9¼" x 9¼" (backgrounds)

Small White Print #2

14 squares 9¼" x 9¼" (backgrounds)

The Blocks (8³/₄" x 8³/₄" finished)

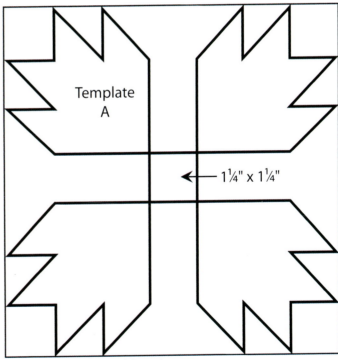

Template for Double Take

Enlarge the pattern 250% until it measures 8³/₄" x 8³/₄". The center square will be 1¼" x 1¼". Add a ¼" seam allowance around the edges for a 9¹/₄" x 9¹/₄" square.

1

Double Take

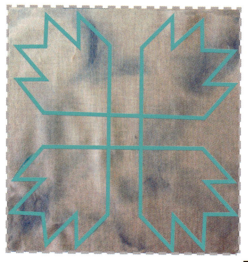

2 Tape the pattern to a light source. Place one of the 9¼" white print background squares with the right-side up directly over the pattern, tape it down, and trace the pattern onto the square using a water-soluble marker. Use a ruler as these lines need to be accurate. Repeat for all 28 blocks.

3 Place a 1¼" medium print square in the center of the block. Press. Place a set of 4 medium print Template A, lining them up with the drawn pattern. Press and machine appliqué, beginning and ending at one of the corners of the 1¼" square. Make a total of 28 blocks.

Assembly

Place the blocks on a wall or floor and decide on an arrangement, setting them 4 blocks across and 7 blocks down. Place a 1¾" x 9¼" medium print sashing between each block. Pin a number to each block to keep track of where each block and each sashing goes in the quilt. Place a 1¾" dark blue square between each sashing piece.

The Borders

Ro
Ro
Ro

Template for Double Take

4 Sew rows 1 and 2 together. Press the seam toward the sashings. Sew rows 3 and 4 together. Continue, until you have all of the rows sewn together in pairs, then join the pairs until the top is assembled.

Use the medium-dark blue and the blue floral strips to create the borders, referring to **Mitered Borders** on page 10 for instructions on how to make and add the mitered borders to the quilt top.

Quilting and Finishing

Make a backing 58" x 88".

Layer the backing, batting and quilt top. Quilt as desired. Trim and square the sandwich. Refer to **Binding** on page 12 to make and apply a double-fold binding. Spritz, rinse or wash the quilt to remove any visible water-soluble markings.

MARBLE MANIA

50" x 50". Made by Joyce Stewart; quilted by Ann Seely.

We grew up in the 1940s and 50s when every grade school kid had a collection of colorful glass and agate marbles. Maybe in years to come, quilts will be named for video games, but for now, this one will help us recall the happy hours of playing marbles.

Marble Mania

Templates

Refer to *Step Three: Make the Templates* under **Machine Appliqué** on page 7 and make a 3" circle and a 2" square template.

Cutting

Fabric

52 assorted bright scrap squares 4¼" x 4¼" (backgrounds)

12 light blue print #1 squares 8" x 8" (backgrounds)

4 dark blue 1½" x 40" strips (inner border)

1 dark blue 3" x 218" strip (binding). Cut and piece the strips together following the **Binding** instructions on page 12.

2 light blue print #2 pieces 42" x 58"
From 1 of these pieces, cut 4 strips 6" x 58" for the outer borders. The leftover fabric will be sewn together to make the backing.

Fusible Web

Refer to *Step Four: Make Fusible-Web Shapes* under **Machine Appliqué** on page 8 for valuable tips.

25 squares 2" x 2" (press to dark blue)
48 circles 3" (press to assorted bright scraps)

The Mania Blocks (7½" x 7½" finished)

Template for Marble Mania

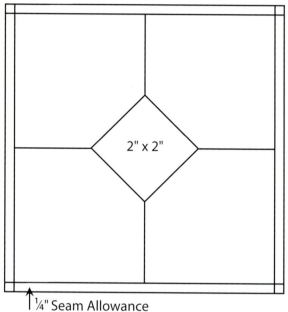

2" x 2"

↑ ¼" Seam Allowance

1 Enlarge the pattern 267% to measure 8" x 8". The center square is 2" x 2".

2 Sew 4 of the 4¼" squares together.

3 Place 1 of the dark blue 2" squares at the center of the block, matching the corners of the square to the seam lines. Press and machine appliqué. Make a total of 13 blocks.

5 Place 4 of the bright scrap 3" circles around the dark blue 2" square, barely touching each circle to the square at the center of each side of the square. Press and stitch. Make a total of 12 blocks.

The Marble Blocks (7½" x 7½" finished)

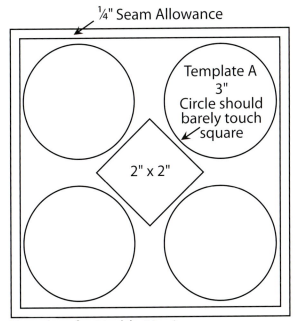

¼" Seam Allowance

Template A
3"
Circle should barely touch square

2" x 2"

Template for Marble Mania

4 Mark the center of each side of the light blue #1 background square with a water-soluble marker. Draw 2 lines on the block from centers to centers. Place one of the dark blue 2" squares in the center of the square, matching the corners of the square to the marked lines. Press and stitch.

Assembly

Sew the blocks together into 5 rows with 5 blocks in each row, alternating Mania and Marble blocks. Sew the rows together.

The Borders

Use the dark blue strips and the light blue print #2 strips to create the borders, referring to **Mitered Borders** on page 10 for instructions on how to make and add the mitered borders to the quilt top.

Quilting and Finishing

Make a backing 58" x 58". Layer the backing, batting and quilt top. Quilt as desired. Trim and square the sandwich. Refer to **Binding** on page 12 to make and apply a 3" double-fold binding. Spritz, rinse or wash the quilt to remove any visible water-soluble markings.

MOTHER'S GIFT

86" x 86". Made and quilted by Ann Seely.

Creating a special quilt for a new bride is a wonderful tradition. It was the same when Mom married Dad in 1937. Mom's mother appliquéd a lovely pansy quilt top and hand-carded the wool for the batting. This was a long process; each carded piece was only about three to six inches long. The area ladies got together to quilt it.

Materials

- 5½ yards cream (background, borders)
- 3 yards lavender (triangle border 1, scallop border, outer border, and binding)
- 1½ yards light green (triangle border 2 and background)
- 2 yards medium green (tulip leaves, stems and corner loops)
- ¼ yard dark blue (joining squares and rectangles)
- ⅛ yard each of 16 assorted pastel prints (rings and tulips)
- 8¼ yards backing
- 7 yards fusible web
- Queen-size quilt batt
- Variegated or matching threads for appliqué
- 3 sheets 8½" x 11" template plastic

Templates

Refer to *Step Three: Make the Templates* under **Machine Appliqué** on page 7 and make templates A, B, C, D, E, F, G, H and I on pages 35–38. For the dark blue joining squares and rectangles, make templates that are 2" square, 1¼" square and a 1¼" x 2" rectangle.

Cutting

Cut and piece the border strips together following the **Mitered Borders** instructions on page 10.

Fabric

Cream

- 4 squares 6½" (backgrounds)
- 16 squares 8½" (backgrounds)
- 2 strips 2" x 48½" (borders)
- 2 strips 2" x 51½" (borders)
- 2 strips 2" x 61½" (borders)
- 2 strips 2" x 64½" (borders)

Light Green

- 28 rectangles 5½" x 7¾" (backgrounds)
- 4 squares 5½" x 5½" (backgrounds)

Lavender

- 4 strips 3½" x the length of the fabric (outer borders)
- 1 strip 3" x 362" for binding. Cut and piece the strips together following the **Binding** instructions on page 12.

Fusible Web

Refer to *Step Four: Make Fusible-Web Shapes* under **Machine Appliqué** on page 8 for valuable tips.

- 128 Template A (press 4 to each pastel print)
- 68 Template B (press 28 to lavender and press 40 to light green)
- 4 Template C (press to lavender)
- 4 Template D (press to lavender)
- 28 Template E (press to lavender)
- 4 Template F (press to lavender)
- 32 Template G (press to medium green)
- 32 Template H (press 2 to each pastel print)
- 4 Template I (press to medium green)
- 4 squares 1¼" (press to dark blue)
- 25 squares 2" x 2" (press to dark blue)
- 12 rectangles 1¼" x 2" (press to dark blue)
- 1 strip 3½" x 22" (press to medium green, then cut the strip into 32 segments ⅜" x 3½" for stems)

The Wedding Ring Blocks (6" x 6" finished)

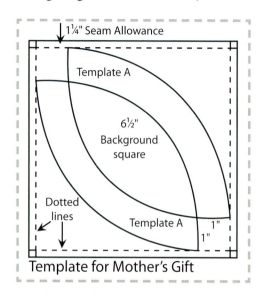

Template for Mother's Gift

1 The templates are on page 37, shown at 100%. Mark a ¼" seam allowance around the outer edge of each cream 6½" x 6½" square.

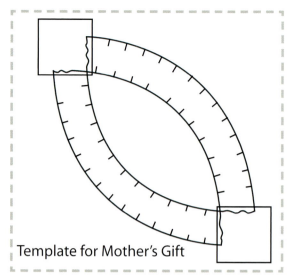

Template for Mother's Gift

3 Place the Template A arcs onto the cream background squares. The arc will overlap slightly into the marked square in the corners. The raw edges will be covered later by the dark blue 2" square. Press and machine appliqué the arcs into place.

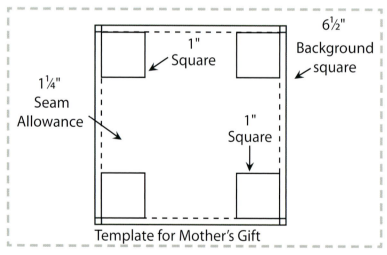

Template for Mother's Gift

2 Mark 1" squares in the corners of the 6½" cream background squares with a water-soluble marker. These will be the reference marks for placing the Template A arcs.

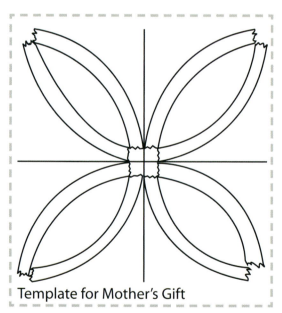

Template for Mother's Gift

4 Lay the 64 blocks into a pleasing arrangement and sew them together into units of 4 blocks each.

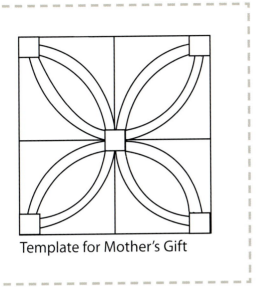

Template for Mother's Gift

The Triangle Border 1

Sew the 2" x 48½" cream borders to the top and bottom of the quilt. Sew the 2" x 51½" cream borders to the sides of the quilt.

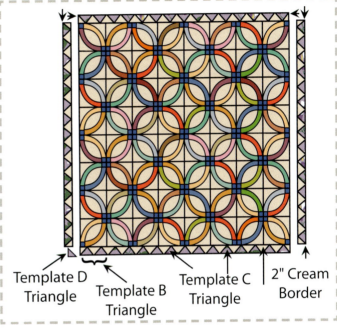

Template D Triangle   Template B Triangle   Template C Triangle   2" Cream Border

5   Place a dark blue 2" square in the center of the 4-block unit, making sure it covers all of the raw edges of the arcs. Press and stitch. Cut away the bulk behind the blue square.

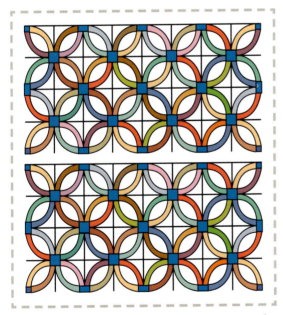

6   Sew the completed units into 4 rows of 4 units each and add the dark blue 2" squares, cutting away the bulk. Add the 12 dark blue 1¼" x 2" rectangles along the sides of the quilt. Add the four 1¼" squares at the corners. Do not cut away behind these pieces.

7   After sewing the cream borders, place a Template D triangle at each corner. Place 7 Template B triangles and 1 Template C triangle along each border. Adjust as necessary to fit, making sure the top tips of all triangles exactly touch the tops of the cream borders. Align the template's long edge with the raw edge of the cream border. Press. Stitch in one long motion around the border triangles.

Mother's Gift

The Scallop Border

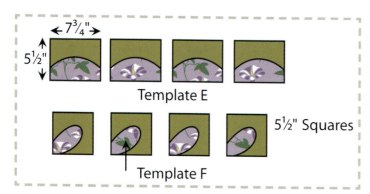

Template E

Template F

5½" Squares

8   Press the 28 lavender Template E scallops to the light green 5½" x 7¾" rectangles and the 4 lavender Template F scallops to the light green 5½" squares. Do not stitch them down yet.

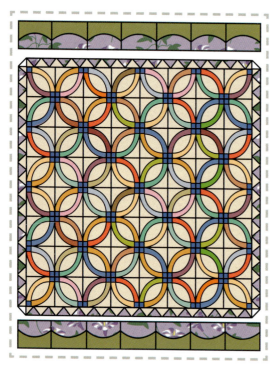

9   Sew 2 rows of 7 light green rectangles that have the Template Es pressed to them. Press the seams open. Stitch the scallops in one long motion. Sew these 2 rows to the top and bottom of the quilt.

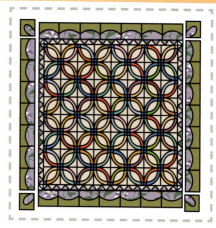

10   Make 2 more rows but add a corner block to the end of each row. Stitch the scallops i one long motion as before. Sew these rows to the sides of the quilt.

The Triangle Border 2

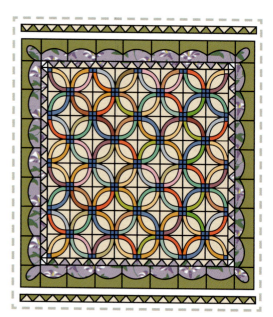

11   Place 10 light green Template B triangles o both 2" x 61½" cream borders, adjusting th triangles to fit evenly along the length of th border, making sure that the top tips of the triangles do not extend into the seam allowance. Press and stitch. Sew these borders to the top and bottom of the quilt.

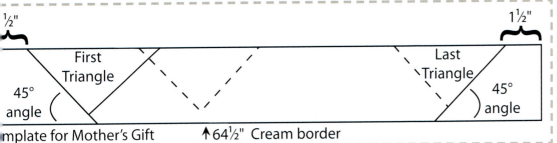

½" 1½"

First Triangle   Last Triangle

45° angle   45° angle

Template for Mother's Gift   ↑ 64½" Cream border

12 Mark the 2" x 64¼" cream borders 1½" from each edge with a water-soluble marker. Mark 45-degree diagonal lines extending from these marks. These will be the reference marks for beginning and ending 10 light green Template B triangles on each of these borders so that they will line up with the side borders properly. Pin and adjust the triangles to fit the borders. Press and stitch. Sew these borders to the sides of the quilt.

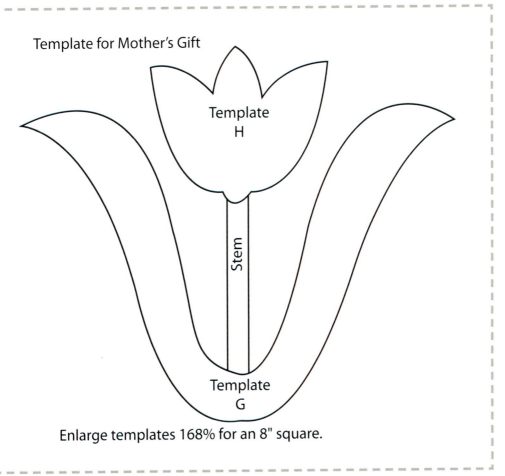

Template for Mother's Gift

Template H

Stem

Template G

Enlarge templates 168% for an 8" square.

13 The block should finish at 8" square. Tape the tulip pattern to a light source. Tape one of the 8½" cream background squares with the right-side up directly over the pattern. Trace the tulip pattern onto the square with a water-soluble marker.

Press a medium green ⅜" x 3½" stem in place and stitch. Place the Template G medium green tulip leaves. Press and stitch. Place the Template H tulip. Press and stitch. Repeat, making 32 Tulip blocks.

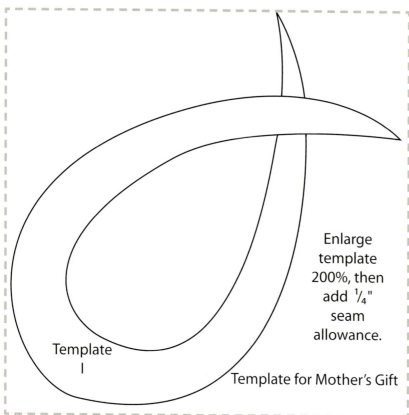

Enlarge
template
200%, then
add $\frac{1}{4}$"
seam
allowance.

Template
I

Template for Mother's Gift

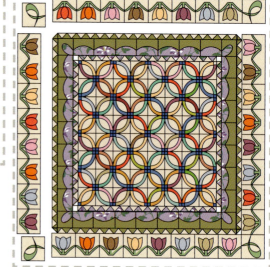

14 Place a medium green Template I corner leaf loop on each of the 4 remaining 8½" cream background squares. Press and stitch.

16 Sew 8 Tulip blocks together. Sew a corner Leaf Loop block to each end of the Tulip block row. Make another row. Sew these rows to the sides of the quilt.

The Outer Border

Use the 4 lavender 3½" strips to create the outer borders. Refer to **Mitered Borders** on page 10 for piecing and sewing instructions.

Quilting and Finishing

Make a 94" x 94" backing. Layer the backing, batting and quilt top. Quilt as desired. Trim and square the sandwich. Refer to **Binding** on page 12 to make and apply a 3" double-fold binding. Spritz, rinse or wash the quilt to remove any visible water-soluble marking.

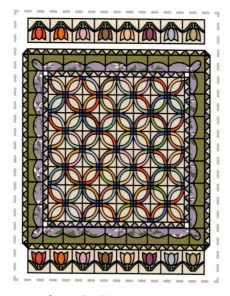

15 Arrange the Tulip blocks as desired. Sew 8 blocks together to form a row. Make a second row. Sew one of these rows to the top of the quilt and one to the bottom of the quilt making sure the tulips face toward the inside of the quilt.

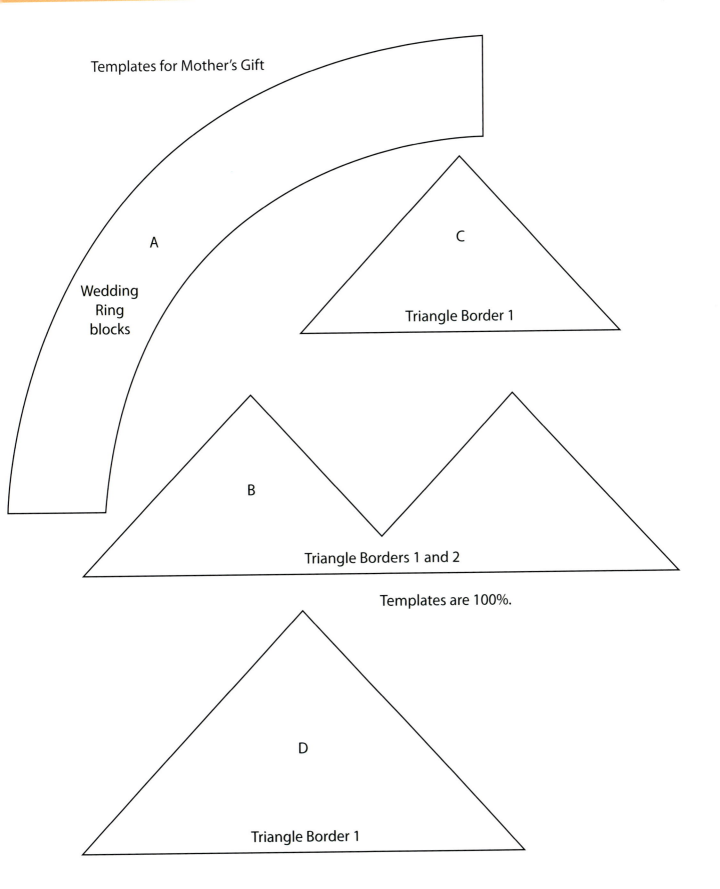

Templates for Mother's Gift

A

Wedding
Ring
blocks

C

Triangle Border 1

B

Triangle Borders 1 and 2

Templates are 100%.

D

Triangle Border 1

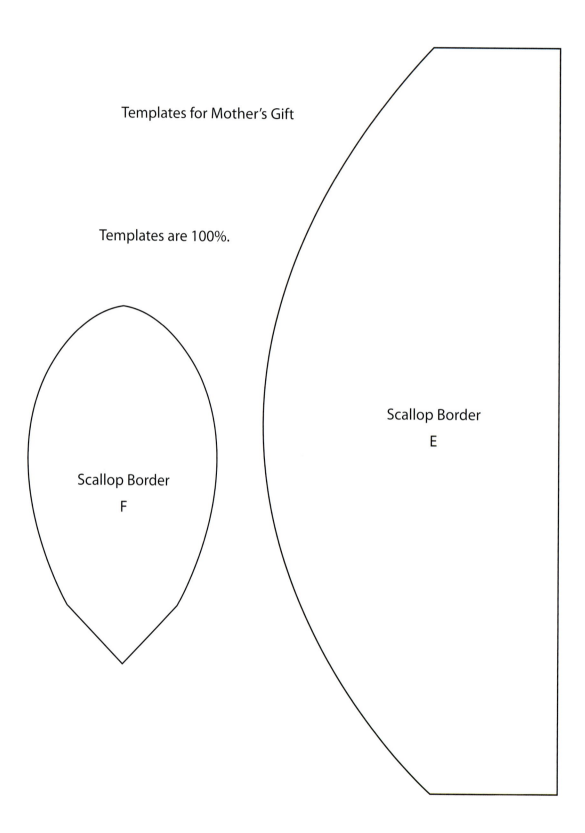

Templates for Mother's Gift

Templates are 100%.

Scallop Border
F

Scallop Border
E

OUR FAVORITE THINGS

44" x 44". Made and quilted by Ann Seely.

The inspiration for this quilt was hiking mountain trails with our grandmother. She would tie ribbons in our hair and we would carry baskets to gather wild chokecherries.

She would point out the different birds and remind us not to pick the wildflowers so that others could enjoy them too.

Materials

- ¼ yard dark peach (background)
- ¼ yard light peach (background)
- ⅛ yard black (basket)
- ⅛ yard green print (basket)
- ⅛ yard yellow print (basket)
- ⅛ yard brown check (basket)
- ¼ yard dark brown print (inner border)
- ⅓ yard light yellow (triangle border)
- 3 ¼ yards green check (outer border, backing and binding)
- 1½ yards large print (corners and triangle border)
- Small scraps of light, medium and dark brown (birds)
- Small scraps of light blue and dark blue (ribbons)
- 1¼ yards fusible web
- 52" x 52" batting
- Thread to match appliqué
- 2 sheets 8½" x 11" template plastic

Templates

Refer to *Step Three: Make the Templates* under **Machine Appliqué** on page 7 and make Templates A, B, C, and D on page 49. Make templates for Birds 1, 2, and 3 and the Bow block on pages 45–48.

Cutting

Fabric

Dark Peach
5 squares 8" (backgrounds)

Light Peach
4 squares 8" (backgrounds)

Brown
2 strips 1¼" x 23" (inner border)
2 strips 1¼" x 24½" (inner border)

Light Yellow
4 strips 2½" x 24½" (triangle border)

Large Print
4 squares 2½" (triangle border)
2 squares 21" x 21" cut in half diagonally (corner triangles)

Green Check
2 rectangles 42" x 54" (outer border, backing and binding)
From one of these pieces, cut 4 strips 3" x 54" for the borders. Then cut 5 strips 3" x 54" for the binding. Set aside the second piece and the piece left from cutting the strips to use for the backing, if you like.

Fusible Web

Refer to *Step Four: Make Fusible-Web Shapes* under **Machine Appliqué** on page 8 for valuable tips.

55 Template A (press 30 to black and press 25 to green print)
5 Template B (press to medium yellow)
5 Template C (press to brown check)
48 Template D (press to the large print)

See the Ribbon and Bird Blocks on page 42 before cutting the fusible for the birds and ribbons.

Once you've read those instructions, cut:

Bird bodies (press to medium brown scraps)
Bird back wings (press to dark brown scraps)
Bird front wings (press to light brown scraps)
Ribbons (press to light blue and dark blue as indicated on the pattern)

The Basket Blocks (7¹/₂" x 7¹/₂" finished)

1 The large pattern on page 49 is shown at 100%.

3 Place the 5 green Template A triangles. Press and stitch.

2 Tape the pattern to a light source. Place one of the 8" dark peach background squares with the right-side up directly over the pattern, tape it down, and trace the pattern onto the square with a water-soluble marker. Following the traced pattern, place 6 black Template A triangles on the background. Press. Machine appliqué around all the triangles in one continuous motion beginning and ending in the same place.

4 Place a yellow Template B basket center. Press and stitch.

5 Place a brown check Template C basket. Press and stitch. Repeat, making 5 Basket blocks.

The Ribbon and Bird Blocks (7½" x 7½" finished)

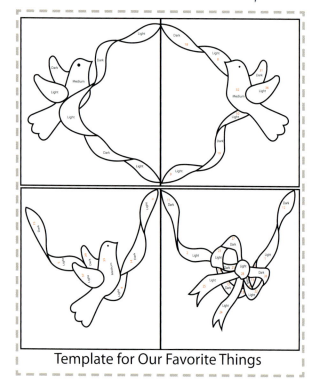

Template for Our Favorite Things

6 The blocks should finish at 7½" square.

Bird A, Bird B, Bird C, Bow

Using a light source, reverse the 4 block patterns and trace all the lines of each pattern with a dark, fine tip marker. Using the reversed drawing of the pattern, trace each shape directly onto the fusible web and label the pieces as shown. Labeling is important since the ribbon shapes will all tend to look alike when they are cut apart.

Tape the pattern right-side up to a light source. Place one of the 8" light peach background squares with the right-side up directly over the pattern, tape it down, and trace the pattern onto the square with a water-soluble marker.

Follow the numbers that indicate the order of pressing and stitching the appliqué. The numbering allows you to press and stitch all the pieces of one color, with a few exceptions. For example, pieces #1 and #2 are light blue; #3, #4 and #5 are also light blue, even though they are on another block.

Repeat, making 3 Bird blocks and 1 Ribbon block.

Template for Our Favorite Things

7 Sew the 5 Basket blocks and the 4 Ribbon and Bird blocks together.

The Inner Borders

Template for Our Favorite Things

8 Sew the 1¼" x 23" dark brown border strips to the top and bottom of the quilt. Sew the 1¼" x 24½" dark brown border strips to the sides of the quilt.

9 Sew the 2½" x 24½" light yellow border strips to the top and bottom of the quilt. Sew a 2½" large print square to each end of the remaining 2 light yellow border strips. Sew these 2 borders to the sides of the quilt.

10 Place 12 large print Template D triangles along one of the light yellow borders, adjusting them to fit. Make sure the tips of the triangles touch just at the seam of the dark brown border. The bottom of the triangles will align with the bottom edge of the light yellow border, extending into the seam allowance. Press and stitch along the top of the triangles only. Repeat for all 4 borders.

The Large Print Triangles

Template for Our Favorite Things

11 Find the center of the large print triangle by folding it in half. Mark the center with a pin. Mark the center of the quilt top. Match the centers and pin and sew the large triangles to the quilt. Sew all 4 corners in the same manner.

The Mitered Border

Referring to **Mitered Borders** on page 10, use the 4 green check 3" x 54" strips to make and add the mitered borders to the quilt top.

Quilting and Finishing

Make a backing 52" x 52". Layer the backing, batting and quilt top. Quilt as desired. Trim and square the sandwich. Refer to **Binding** on page 12 to make and apply a 3" double-fold binding. Spritz, rinse or wash the quilt to remove any visible water-soluble markings.

Our Favorite Things

Template for Our Favorite Things

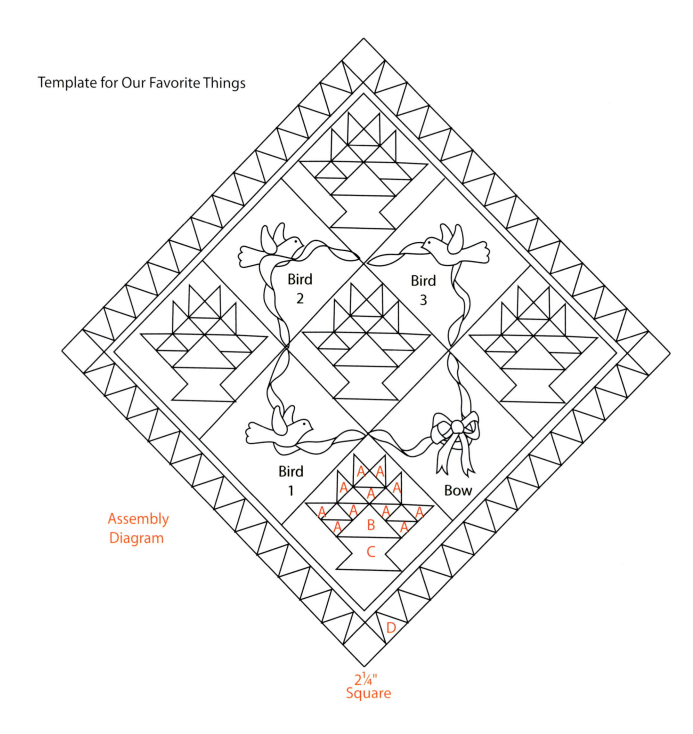

Bird 2

Bird 3

Bird 1

Bow

Assembly Diagram

A A
A A
A A A A A
A A B A
C
D

2¼"
Square

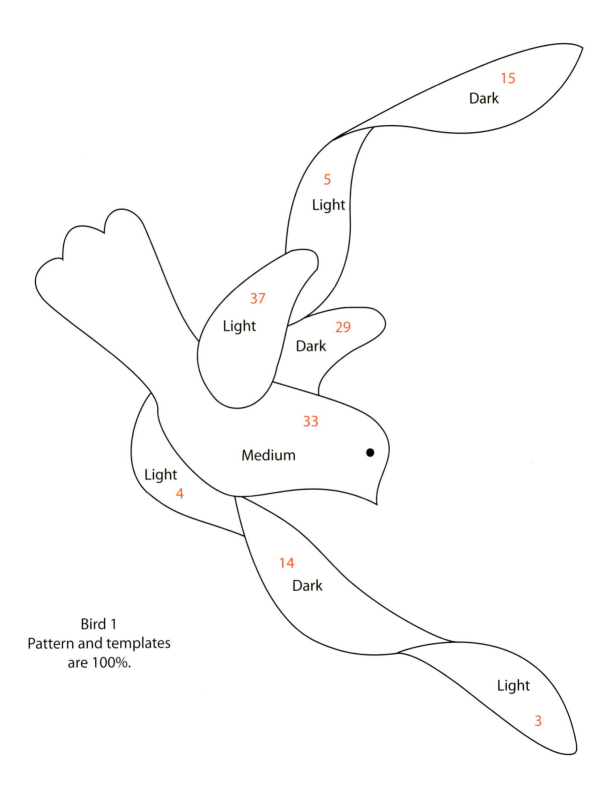

15
Dark

5
Light

37
Light

29
Dark

33
Medium

Light
4

14
Dark

Bird 1
Pattern and templates
are 100%.

Light
3

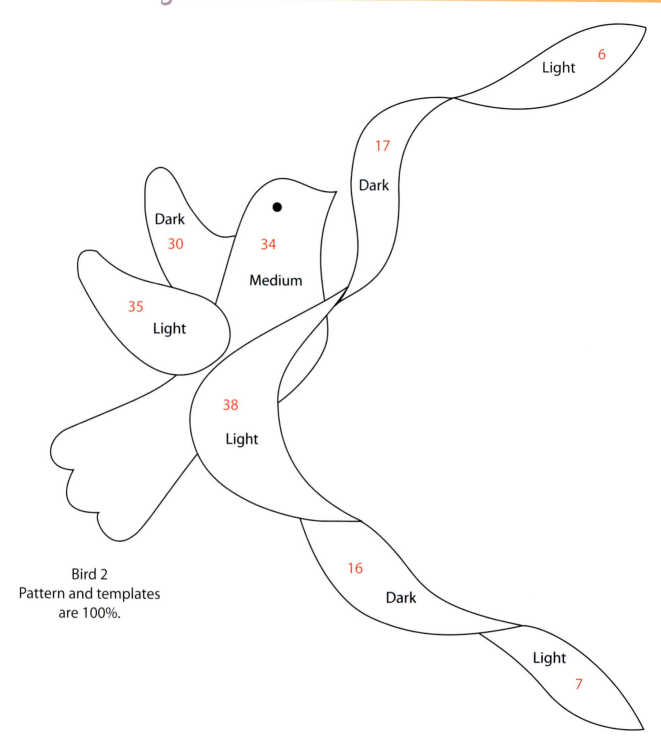

Light 6

17
Dark

Dark
30

34
Medium

35
Light

38
Light

Bird 2
Pattern and templates
are 100%.

16
Dark

Light
7

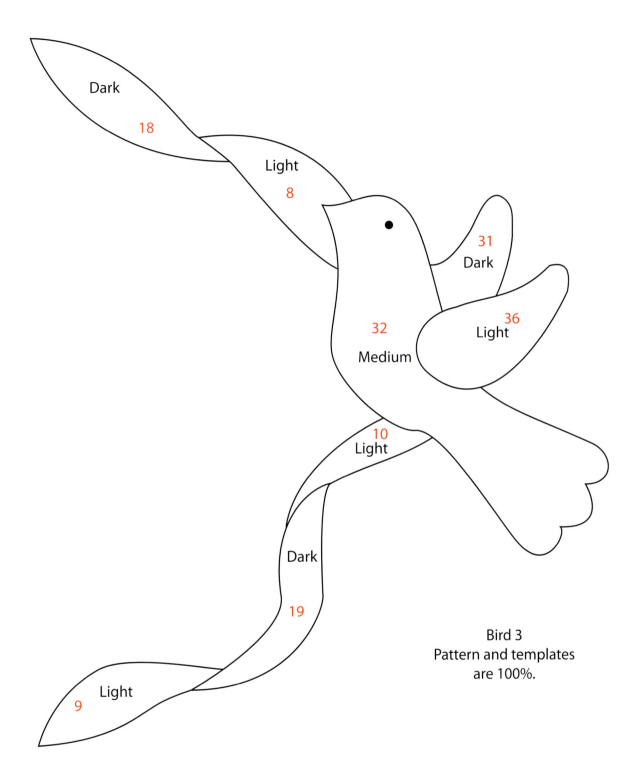

Dark

18

Light

8

31
Dark

32

36
Light

Medium

10
Light

Dark

19

Bird 3
Pattern and templates
are 100%.

Light

9

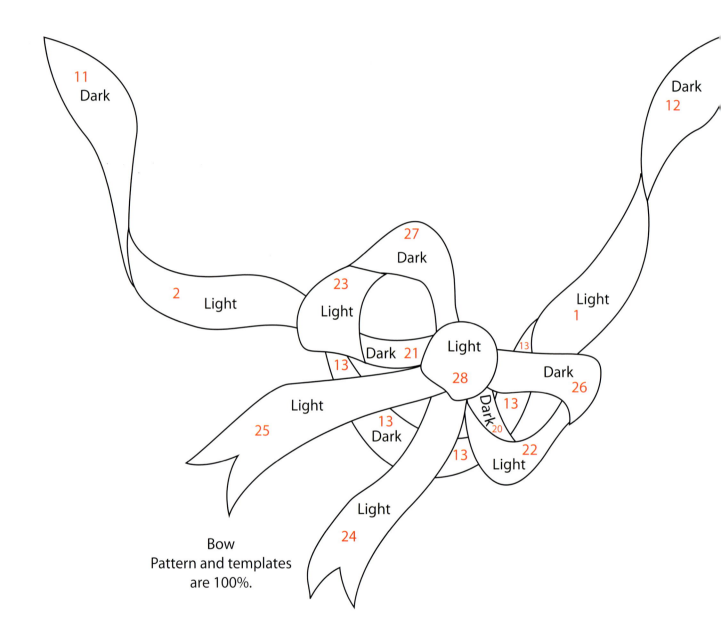

11
Dark

Dark
12

27
Dark

23
Light

2
Light

Light
1

13

Dark 21

Light
28

13

Dark
26

13

Dark

13

Light

Light
25

13
Dark

13

Dark
20

13

22
Light

Light
24

Bow
Pattern and templates
are 100%.

d ¼" seam allowance

Templates are 100%.

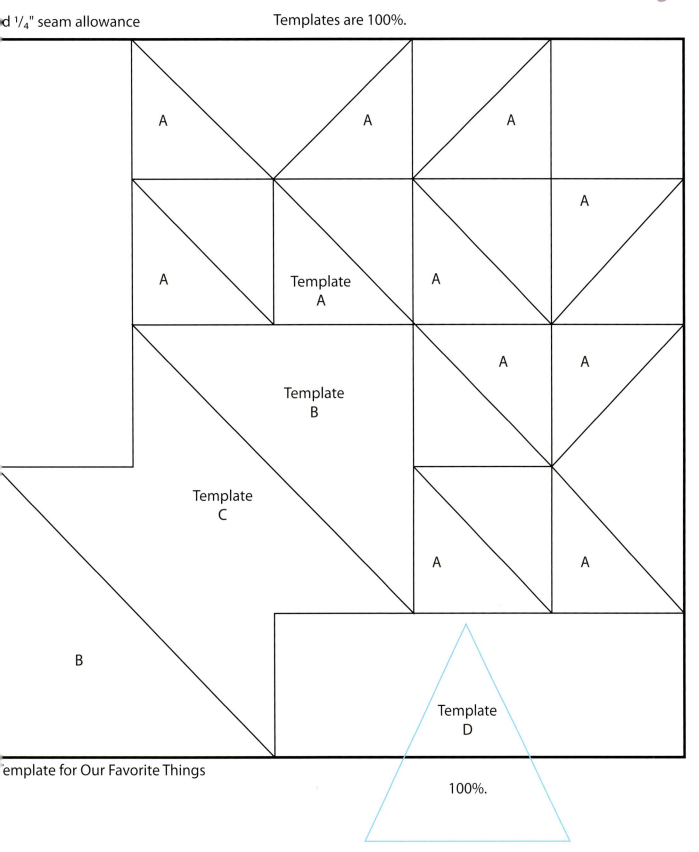

A

A

A

A

A

A

Template
A

A

Template
B

A

A

Template
C

A

A

B

Template
D

100%.

Template for Our Favorite Things

RAPUNZEL'S WINDOW

23" x 23". Made and quilted by Ann Seely.

As quiltmakers, we can let fabric transport us to another world—as in a fairy tale—where our points are perfect, our corners square, our seams lie flat, and all our witches are just skipped stitches. Who knows, maybe our fairy godmother really is looking out for us! And what makes a happier ending than finishing a wonderful quilt?

Materials

⅞ yard busy print (background, borders and binding)

10" square blue check (background)

⅛ yard medium blue (inner border)

10" square light yellow

6" square (picture motif which must fit nicely into a 4⅛" octagon)

¼ yard dark purple

¼ yard medium yellow (2nd border)

¼ yard light blue (mitered border)

¼ yard pink (mitered border)

¾ yard backing

¾ yard fusible web

27" x 27" thin batting

Variegated or matching threads for appliqué

1 sheet 8½" x 11" template plastic

Templates

Refer to *Step Three: Make the Templates* under **Machine Appliqué** on page 7 and make Templates A, B, C, D, and E on page 55.

Cutting

Fabric

Busy Print

busy print 10½" x 10½" (square)

strips 2¼" x 26" (outer border)

strip 3" x 104" (binding). Cut and piece the strips together following the **Binding** instructions on page 12.

Blue Check

squares 3⅜" x 3⅜" (background)

Medium Blue

strips 1½" x 10 ½" strips (inner border top and bottom)

strips 1½" x 12½" strips (inner border sides)

Medium Yellow

2 strips 2½" x 12½" (2ⁿᵈ border top and bottom)

2 strips 2½" x 16½" (2ⁿᵈ border sides)

Pink

4 strips 1¼" x 26" strips (3ʳᵈ border)

Light blue

4 strips 1¾" x 26" (final border)

Fusible Web

Refer to *Step Four: Make Fusible-Web Shapes* under **Machine Appliqué** on page 8 for valuable tips.

1 Template A (press to light yellow)

1 Template B (press to motif, centering motif)

8 Template C (press to dark purple)

16 Template D (press to blue)

20 Template E (press to dark purple)

The Center (10" x 10" finished)

1   The templates on page 55 are 100%. See page 54 for placement diagram.

The Borders

2 Align the 4 blue check 3⅜" squares right sides together with the corners of the 10½" busy print background square. Draw a diagonal line; sew along the line. Press and trim the excess fabric ¼" past the stitching.

Fold the block in half twice and finger press to mark the center. This will be the reference mark for centering the light yellow Template A octagon. Place the octagon, making sure the centers are lined up and the straight lines of the octagon follow the lines of the block. Press and stitch.

4 Sew the 1½" x 10 ½" medium blue border strips to the top and bottom of the block. Sew the 1½" x 12½" medium blue border strips to the sides of the block.

3 Trim the extra fabric from behind the light yellow octagon. Find the center as before and draw lines to use as reference marks for lining up the Template B motif. Place the motif. Press and stitch.

5 Place the purple Template C diamond shapes. The inner tip of the diamond shoul. touch the points of the motif octagon and the outer tips should touch the points of th. print octagon, but should not go into the blue borders. Press and machine appliqué.

6 Sew the 2½" x 12½" medium yellow border strips to the top and bottom of the quilt. Sew the 2½" x 16½" medium yellow border strips to the sides of the quilt.

Refer to **Mitered Borders** on page 10 for instructions on how to make and add a mitered border to the quilt top. Sew the light blue, pink and busy print top border strips together to create the borders.

The Appliqué

7 Place 4 blue Template D triangles exactly along one edge of the yellow border, making sure the tips of the triangles do not go into the seam allowance of the busy print border. Repeat for each side. Press and stitch the triangles, stitching the long straight edge of the triangles first.

8 Place the dark purple Template E pieces. The points of Template E should align along the seam line between the pink fabric and the busy blue print. The tips of the Template E pieces should not extend into the seam allowance of the outer border. Press and stitch.

Quilting & Finishing

Make a backing 27" x 27".

Layer the backing, batting and quilt top. Quilt as desired. Trim and square the sandwich. Refer to **Binding** on page 12 to make and apply a 3" double-fold binding. Spritz, rinse or wash the quilt to remove any visible water-soluble markings.

Embellishing

9   Now you can have fun embellishing! Sew beads to the edge of the binding and add "fairy tale" sparkle by adding tiny crystals or any other kinds of embellishments that suit your fancy. Search the Internet or your local craft stores to find beads, crystals, etc., that will add another dimension to your work, even fabric paint as shown.

Shown before fabric paint was applied.

Placement Diagram
Letter=template

Templates for Our Favorite Things

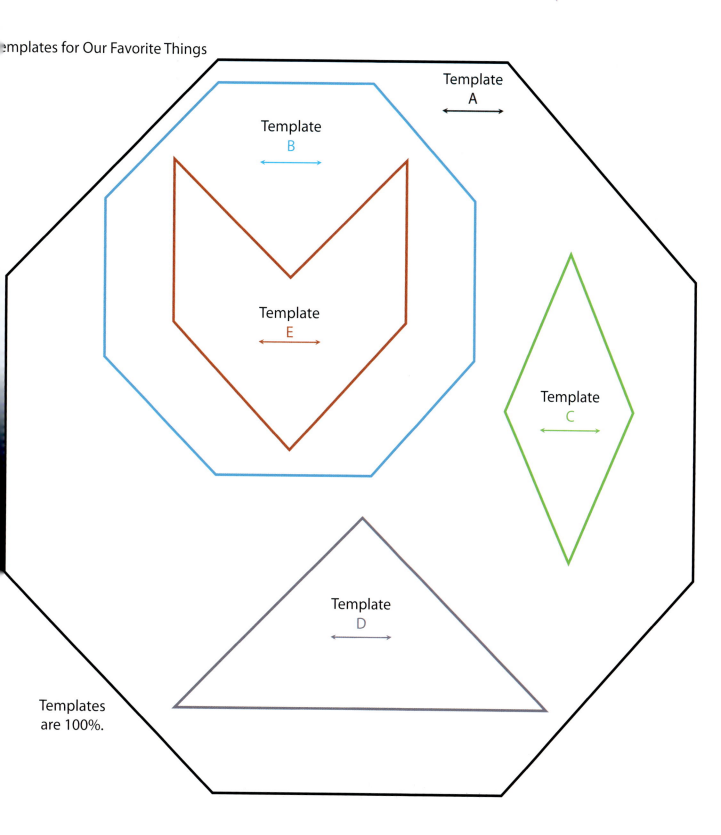

Template
A

Template
B

Template
E

Template
C

Template
D

Templates
are 100%.

SCRAPPY PINWHEELS

86" x 86". Made by Joyce Stewart; quilted by Ann Seely.

One year we vacationed in Hawaii with Mom and Dad and went to a Muu Muu factory. While we looked at dresses, Mom asked the owner if he had any fabric for sale. He replied, "No, but there are scraps in the barrels you can have for free." We filled bags with enough scraps for each of us to make a queen-sized quilt when we got home.

Materials

3¾ yards assorted light scraps (background)
3¾ yards assorted dark scraps (background)
3 yards assorted medium scraps (pinwheels)
2⅝ yards medium green (outer border)
1 yard medium-dark green (middle border)
1½ yards dark green (inner border and
   binding)
8¼ yards backing
6 yards fusible web
Queen-size quilt batt
Variegated thread for appliqué
1 sheet 8½" x 11" template plastic

Templates

Refer to *Step Three: Make the Templates* under
Machine Appliqué on page 7 and make Template A on
page 60.

Cutting

Cut and piece the border strips together following the
Mitered Borders instructions on page 10.

Fabric

Dark scraps
40 squares 6" x 6" (insides of blocks)
82 squares 6" x 6" cut in half diagonally
   to make 164 triangles (outsides
   of blocks)

Light scraps
41 squares 6" x 6" (insides of blocks)
80 squares 6" x 6" cut in half diagonally
   to make 160 triangles (outsides
   of blocks)

Dark green
4 strips 1¾" x 72" (inner border)
1 strip 3" x 362" (binding). Cut and piece
   the strips together following the **Binding**
   instructions on page 12.

Medium-dark green
4 strips 3½" x 76" (middle border)

Medium green
4 strips 7" x 90" (outer border)

Fusible Web

Refer to *Step Four: Make Fusible-Web Shapes* under
Machine Appliqué on page 8 for valuable tips.

324 Template A (press to assorted medium scraps in
   sets of 4)

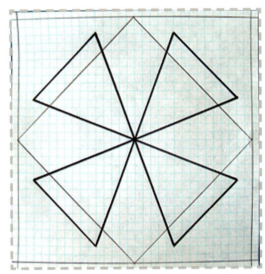

1. The block should measure 8" square and finish at 7½" square. Make 81 copies of the block pattern on page 60. Be sure that the copy machine you are using makes an accurate copy before making all of the copies of the pattern. Do not trim the paper copies to size at this time. They will be trimmed to size after sewing the fabric to the paper.

2 Lay a 6" dark scrap square in the center of a paper pattern on the wrong side of the paper. Secure with a pin or dab of glue. Make sure the fabric extends at least ¼" past the lines of the marked square for seam allowance.

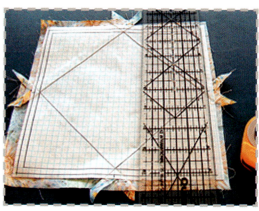

4 Repeat for the next 2 light scrap triangles. Trim the block from the right side of the paper on the 8" block line, making sure the seam line doesn't get cut off. The block should measure 8" square. Tear away the paper.

3 Place 2 of the light scrap triangles on opposite sides of the square on top of the dark scrap square with right sides together. Stitch from the **right** side of the paper exactly on the marked stitching lines. Make small stitches. Begin and end stitching at least ½" outside of the 8" block lines. Press seams.

5 Tape the pattern to a light source. Place the block with the right-side up directly over the pattern, tape it down, and trace the pattern onto the block. Use a water-soluble marker for the light scraps and a white chalk pencil for the dark scraps. Make a mark in the center of the block.

6 Place 4 Template A of the same fabric on the block making sure the points are exactly in the center and on the marked lines. Press and machine appliqué, beginning and ending in the center. Make 40 blocks using the dark scraps for the center squares and the light scraps for the outside triangles.

The Blocks
Assembly

Sew the blocks together into 9 rows of 9 blocks, alternating the light center and dark center blocks. The corner blocks should have light scrap centers and dark scrap outside triangles.

The Borders

Refer to **Mitered Borders** on page 10 for instructions on how to make and add a mitered border to the quilt top. Sew the dark green, medium-dark green, and medium green border strips together to create the borders.

Quilting and Finishing

Make a 94" x 94" backing. Layer the backing, batting and quilt top. Quilt as desired. Trim and square the sandwich. Refer to **Binding** on page 12 to make and apply a 3" double-fold binding. Spritz, rinse or wash the quilt to remove any visible water-soluble markings.

7 Make 41 blocks using the light scraps as the center squares and the dark scraps for the outside triangles.

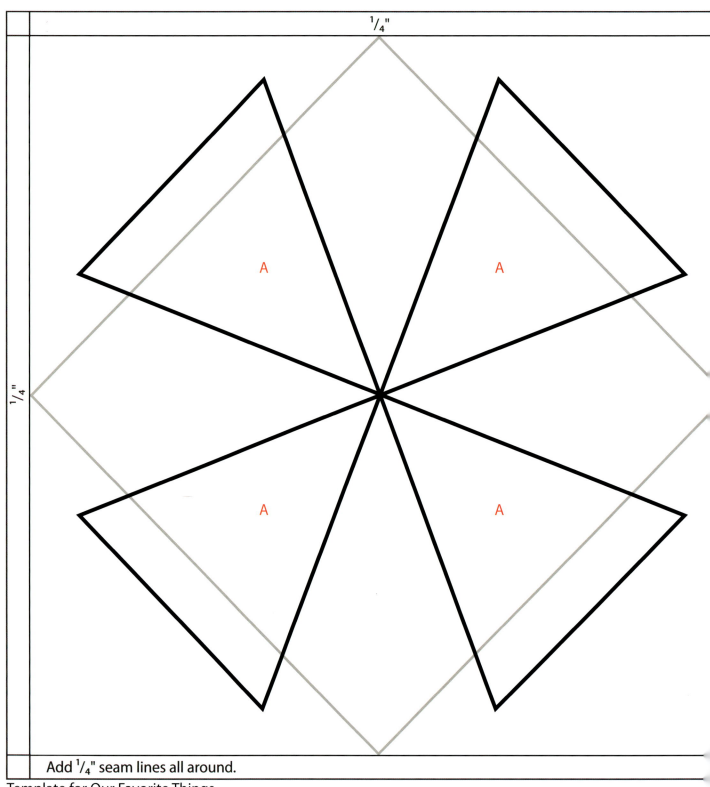

¹/₄"

¹/₄"

A

A

A

A

Add ¹/₄" seam lines all around.

Template for Our Favorite Things

Pattern and template are 100%.

SUMMER FUN

54" x 78". Made by Joyce Stewart; quilted by Ann Seely.

A carnival came through town every summer when we were young. The empty field where it set up became a brightly colored wonderland of Ferris wheels, bumper cars, carousels, and cotton candy. We'll never forget the summer fun of the carnival.

Materials

- 2¾ yards medium-dark blue (background and binding)
- ¾ yard blue stripe (blocks)
- ¾ yard yellow-orange stripe (blocks)
- ⅛ yard each of 9 assorted large prints (pinwheels)
- ⅛ yard each of 9 assorted small prints (pinwheels)
- ½ yard green (inner border)
- ⅜ yard orange (middle border)
- 2⅛ yards blue print (outer border)
- 3⅜ yards backing
- 2 yards fusible web
- Twin-size quilt batt
- Variegated thread for appliqué
- 1 sheet 8 ½" x 11" template plastic

Templates

Refer to *Step Three: Make the Templates* under **Machine Appliqué** on page 7 and make Templates A, B, and C on page 65 and a 5½" square template.

Cutting

Cut and piece the border strips together following the **Mitered Borders** instructions on page 10.

Fabric

Medium-dark Blue
15 squares 12½" x 12½" (backgrounds)
1 strip 3" x 282" (binding). Cut and piece the strips together following the **Binding** instructions on page 12.

Green
2 strips 2" x 42" (top and bottom borders)
2 strips 2" x 67" (side borders)

Orange
2 strips 1¾" x 45" (top and bottom borders)
2 strips 1¾" x 69" (side borders)

Blue print
2 strips 7" x 60" (top and bottom borders)
2 strips 7" x 83" (side borders)

Blue stripe
16 squares 5½" x 5½"

Yellow-orange stripe
14 squares 5½" x 5½"

1 Trace and cut the required squares onto the striped fabrics using the 5½" square template, making sure the length of the stripe is on the diagonal. Cut each striped square into 2 triangles, following the pattern of the stripe.

Fusible Web

Refer to *Step Four: Make Fusible-Web Shapes* under **Machine Appliqué** on page 8 for valuable tips.

60 Template A (press to assorted large print fabrics in sets of 4)
60 Template B (press to assorted small print fabrics in sets of 4)

Making the Blocks (12" x 12" finished)

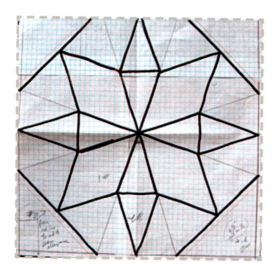

2 Enlarge the pattern on page 65 185% to measure 12½" x 12½". Templates A, B, and C are 100%. The block should finish at 12" square. Make 8 blocks using the blue striped fabric and 7 blocks using the yellow-orange striped fabric.

4 Using a plastic ruler and a rotary cutter, cut along the marked line on each square.

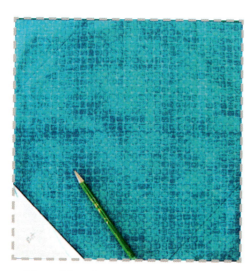

3 Using Template C, mark on the wrong side of the medium-dark blue 12½" square at each corner by drawing a line along the edge of the triangle.

5 Take 4 striped triangles of the same color and place them right sides together along the trimmed edges of the block. Sew with an exact ¼" seam. Press the seam towards the outside of the block. *Sew and press carefully as the block edges are now on the bias of the fabric.*

6 Trim the striped fabric and square the block to 12½".

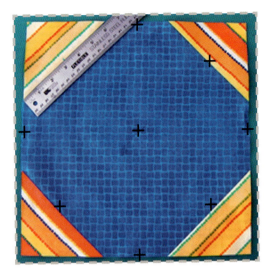

7 On the right side, mark the center of the block, and mark the center along the outside edges. Mark the center of the long edge of each striped triangle.

9 Place a set of 4 small-print Template B triangles onto the block. Line up these triangle pieces using the side points of the diamonds and the center of the block along the outside edges, allowing for ¼" seam allowances on the edges. Press and stitch.

Assembly

Sew the blocks together alternating the blue striped blocks and the yellow-orange striped blocks. Make 5 rows with 3 blocks in each row. The corner blocks should be blue striped blocks.

The Borders

Refer to **Mitered Borders** on page 10 for instructions on how to make and add a mitered border to the quilt top. Sew the shorter green, orange and blue print border strips together to create the top and bottom borders. Sew the longer strips together for the side borders.

8 Place a set of 4 large-print Template A diamonds onto the block, using the mark in the center of the block and the center of the long edge of each striped triangle to line up these diamond pieces. Press and machine appliqué, beginning and ending in the center of the diamonds.

Quilting and Finishing

Make a backing 62" x 86". Layer the backing, batting and quilt top. Quilt as desired. Trim and square the sandwich. Refer to **Binding** on page 12 to make and apply a 3" double-fold binding. Spritz, rinse or wash the quilt to remove any visible water-soluble markings.

Template for Summer Fun

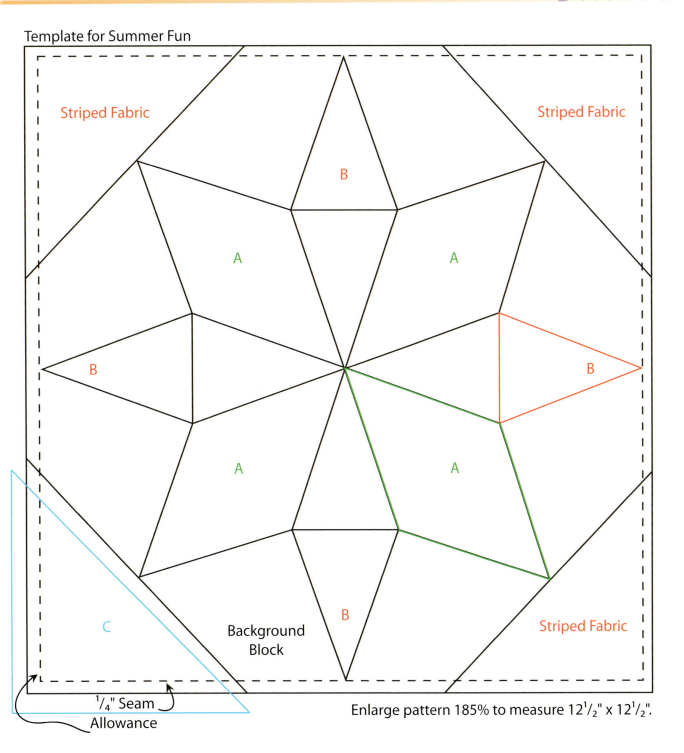

Striped Fabric

Striped Fabric

B

A

A

B

B

A

A

Striped Fabric

C

Background
Block

B

$^1/_4$" Seam
Allowance

Enlarge pattern 185% to measure 12$^1/_2$" x 12$^1/_2$".

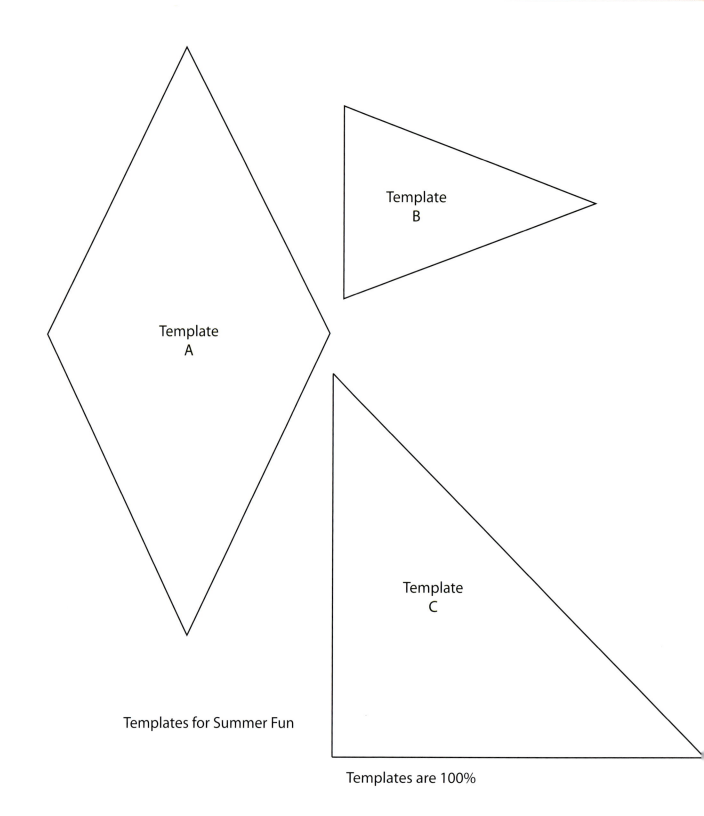

Template
A

Template
B

Template
C

Templates for Summer Fun

Templates are 100%

TREASURES

32" x 32". Made by Joyce Stewart; quilted by Ann Seely.

After our parents passed away we sorted through rooms of items accumulated through Mom and Dad's lifetimes. When we came across a stack of old photo albums, all the work stopped and we spent hours laughing and remembering and realizing that our most valuable treasures were our memories.

Materials

- *(Fabric letters correspond to the assembly diagram on page 71. Unless otherwise identified, all fabrics were used in making the blocks.)*

- ¼ yard light yellow (ly) (background)
- ¼ yard light gold (lg)
- ⅔ yard gold (g) (background and Template N)
- ⅛ yard gold plaid (gpld)
- ¼ yard light green (lgr)
- ⅝ yard medium-light green (mlgr) (outer border)
- ¼ yard medium green (mgr)
- ½ yard medium-dark green (mdgr) (binding)
- ¼ yard black plaid (bpld)
- ⅛ yard dark red print (dkrp)
- ¼ yard dark red (dr) (inner border)
- 1 yard backing
- 2½ yards fusible web
- 40" x 40" thin batting
- Matching threads for appliqué
- 1 sheet 8½" x 11" template plastic

Templates

(Template letters refer to illustration 3 on page 69.)

Refer to *Step Three: Make the Templates* under **Machine Appliqué** on page 7 and make Templates A, B, C, and N on page 77. Make templates that are 1¼" square, 1¾" square, 2½" square and 3½" square. Also, make one rectangular template in each of the following sizes:

Template D/E	1¼" x 2½"
Template F/G	1⅜" x 2¾"
Template H/I	1½" x 3"
Template J/K	1½" x 2¾"
Template L/M	1⅝" x 3⅛"

1 Draw a rectangle the size you need onto the fusible web. Use a ruler and draw a line from bottom left to top right. Templates D, F, H, J, and L must be drawn in this direction.

2 Draw a rectangle in the size you need onto the fusible web. Use a ruler and draw a line from top left to bottom right. Templates E, G, I, K, and M must be drawn in this direction.

Note Each rectangle will make 2 triangle shapes. This is taken into account in the cutting. Label each triangle shape to eliminate confusion.

Cutting

Fabric

1 gold square 10½" x 10½" (background Block 1)
4 gold rectangles 8" x 10½" (background Block 2)
4 light yellow squares 8" x 8" (background Block 3)
4 dark red strips 1¼" x width of fabric (inner border)

4 medium-light green strips 4" x width of fabric (outer border)
1 strip medium-dark green 3" x 140" (binding). Cut and piece strips together following the **Binding** instructions on page 12.

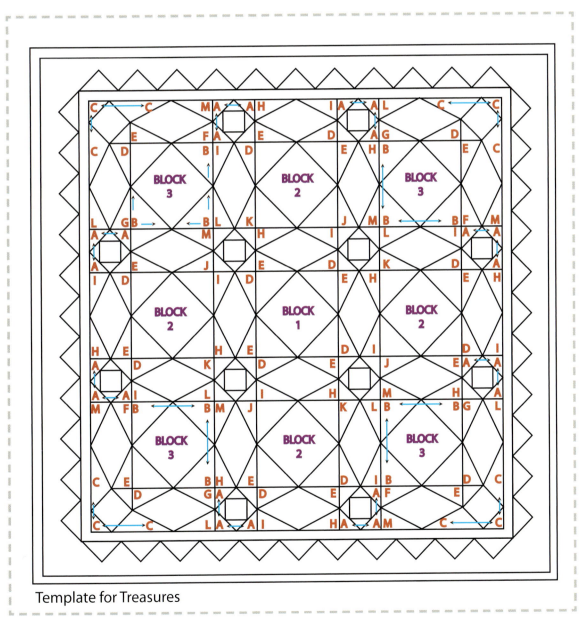

Template for Treasures

3   Pattern and template layout

Cutting

Fusible Web

Refer to *Step Four: Make Fusible-Web Shapes* under **Machine Appliqué** on page 8 for valuable tips.

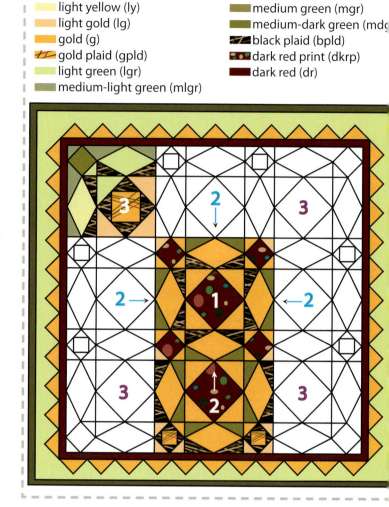

light yellow (ly)
light gold (lg)
gold (g)
gold plaid (gpld)
light green (lgr)
medium-light green (mlgr)
medium green (mgr)
medium-dark green (mdg
black plaid (bpld)
dark red print (dkrp)
dark red (dr)

The Blocks

Block 1 (10" x 10" finished)

1 square 3½" x 3½" (press to dark red print)
4 squares 1¾" x 1¾" (press to dark red print)
4 squares 1½" x 1½" (press to light gold)
4 Template D (press to black plaid)
4 Template E (press to black plaid)
4 Template H (press to medium green)
4 Template I (press to medium green)

Block 2 (7¹/₂" x 10" finished)

4 squares 3½" x 3½" (press to dark red print)
8 squares 1¾" x 1¾" (press to black plaid)
8 squares 1¼" x 1¼" (press to gold plaid)
8 Template A (press to light gold)
8 Template D (press to medium green)
8 Template E (press to medium green)
8 Template H (press to black plaid)
8 Template I (press to black plaid)
4 Template J (press to medium green)
4 Template K (press to medium green)
4 Template L (press to black plaid)
4 Template M (press to black plaid)

Block 3 (7¹/₂" x 7¹/₂" finished)

4 squares 3½" x 3½" (press to black plaid)
4 squares 2½" x 2½" (press to gold plaid)
4 squares 1¾" x 1¾" (press to medium green)
4 Template B (press to light gold)
4 Template C (press to light green)
4 Template D (press to black plaid)
4 Template E (press to black plaid)
4 Template F (press black plaid)
4 Template G (press to black plaid)
4 Template L (press to light green)
4 Template M (press to light green)

Border

52 Template N (press to gold)

Enlarge pattern 35% to measure 10" x 10".

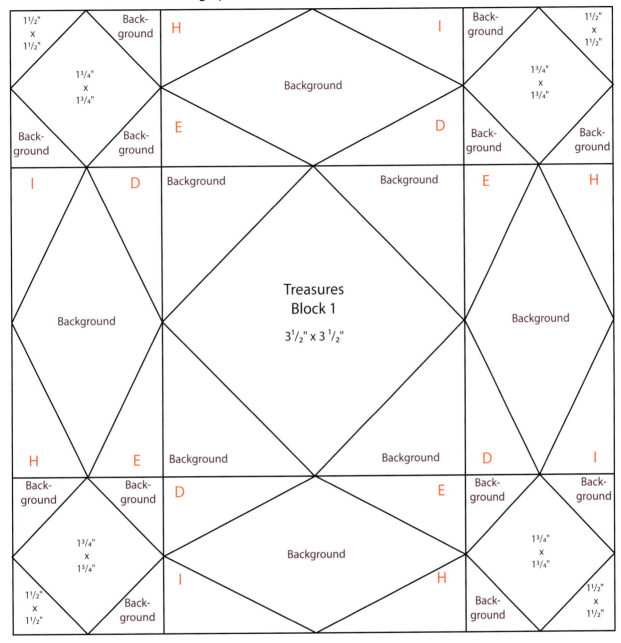

5 After the pattern is enlarged add ¼" seam allowance to the block. Tape the pattern to a light source. Place the 10½" gold background square with the right-side up directly over the pattern, tape it down, and trace the pattern onto the square using a water-soluble marker.

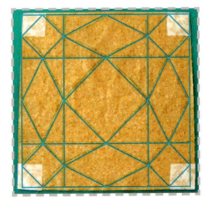

6 Place the 4 light gold 1½" squares at the corners of the block, keeping the edges flush. Press, but do not stitch. These will be partially covered and fully secured by the dark red print 1¾" squares later.

Block 1 finished

7 Working from the center to the outside, place a 3½" dark red square in the center. Press and machine appliqué. Place 4 black plaid Template D and 4 black plaid Template E. Press and stitch. Place 4 medium green Template H and 4 medium green Template I around the outside edges. Press and stitch, except along the outside edges. These triangles will overlap at the center of each side. Press the 4 dark red print 1¾" squares in the corners, leaving a ¼" seam allowance. Stitch.

Block 2 (7½" x 10" finished)

Enlarge the pattern 30% to measure 7½" x 10".

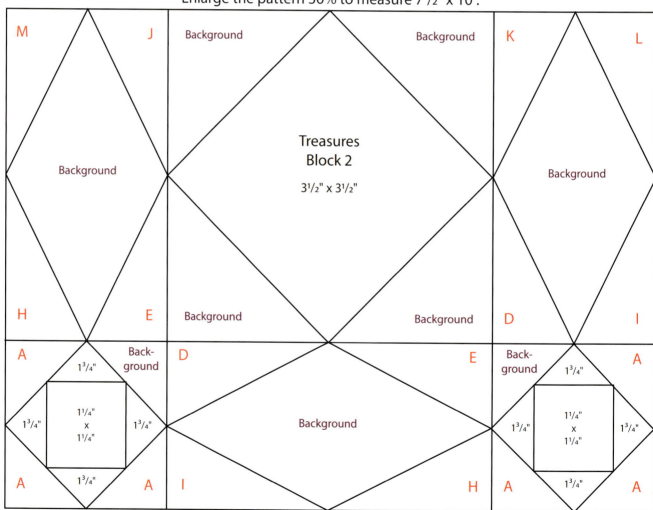

8 After the block is enlarged, add ¼" seam allowance to the block. Tape the pattern to a light source. Place an 8" x 10½" gold background rectangle with the right-side up directly over the pattern, tape it down, and trace the pattern onto the rectangle using a water-soluble marker.

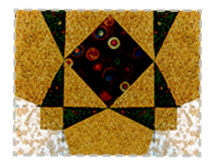

9   Place 2 light gold Template A in the corners of the block. Press, but do not stitch. Make marks going out from the corner on each side of the light gold at 1½" and 2¾" to use as placement guides. Place a 3½" dark red square. Press and stitch. Place 2 medium green Template D and 2 medium green Template E. Place a medium green Template J and a medium green Template K. Press and stitch.

Block 2 finished

10   Place 2 black plaid Template H and 2 black plaid Template I following the lines and matching the large outside edge of the triangle with the 2¾" marks. Place a black plaid Template L and a black plaid Template M. Press and stitch, except along the outside edges. These triangles will overlap at the center of each side. Place 2 black plaid 1¾" squares over the light gold, matching the points of the square and the triangles and having the outside points of the square lined up with the 1½" mark, leaving a ¼" seam allowance. Press and stitch. Place 2 gold plaid 1¼" squares on top of the black plaid 1¾" squares. Press and stitch. Repeat to make 4 of Block 2.

Block 3 (7½" x 7½" finished)

Pattern is 100%. 7½" x 7½".

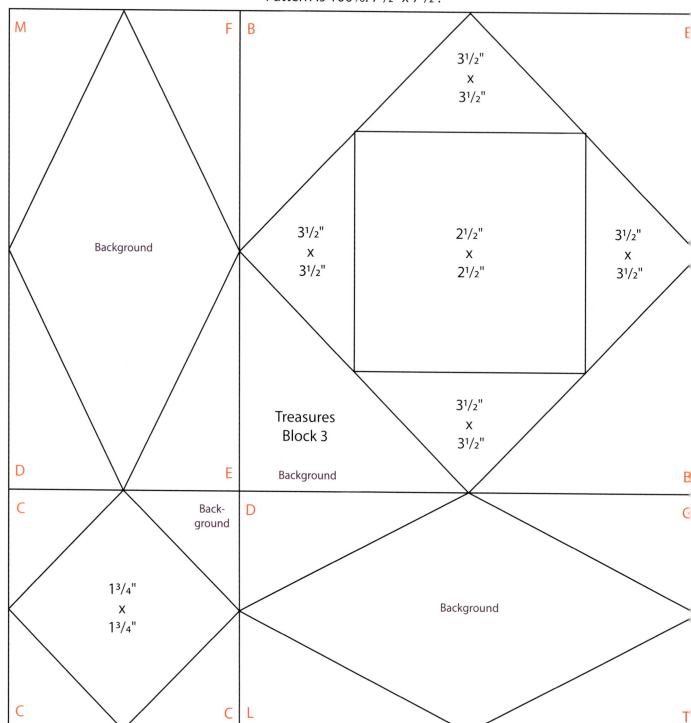

M   F | B   E

Background

3½" x 3½"

3½" x 3½"   2½" x 2½"   3½" x 3½"

Treasures Block 3

3½" x 3½"

Background

D   E

C   Back-ground | D

1¾" x 1¾"

Background

C   C | L

11 After the block is enlarged, add ¼" seam allowance to the block. Tape the pattern to a light source. Place an 8" x 8" light yellow background square with the right-side up directly over the pattern, tape it down, and trace the pattern onto the square using a water-soluble marker.

12 Place a light gold Template B at the corner of the block. Press, but do not stitch. Make marks going out from the corner on each side of the light gold at 2¾" and 5¼" to use as placement guides. Place a light green Template C at the opposite corner of the block. Place a light green Template L and a light green Template M. Press and stitch, except along the outside edges. These triangles will overlap at the center of each side. Place a black plaid Template D and a black plaid Template E. Press and stitch. Make marks going out from the corner on each side of the light green at 1½" for placement guides.

13 Place a black plaid Template F and a black plaid Template G, lining up the triangle edges at the 5¼" mark. Press and stitch, except along the outside edges. Place a 3½" black plaid square, matching corners to the 2¾" marks and at center of black plaid triangles, leaving ¼" for seam allowance on the light gold. Press and stitch. Place a 2½" gold plaid square over the black plaid square. Press and stitch. Place a 1¾" medium green square, matching the 1½" marks and the points of the black plaid triangles, leaving ¼" for seam allowance on the light green. Press and stitch.

Repeat to make 4 of Block 3.

14 Assemble in 3 rows.

Block 3 finished

Note After sewing the blocks and the rows together, do a machine appliqué stitch on the triangle edges that are not already machine appliquéd.

Border Triangles

15   Place 13 gold Template N triangles along each side of the quilt, placing the long edges of the triangles exactly flush with the seam between the dark red and the medium-light green border. Start and end exactly at the corner's edge. You may have to adjust your triangles slightly, moving some closer together or some further apart to make them fit. Press carefully, a few at a time, making sure they don't shift. Machine appliqué. Note: After stitching, slight adjustments will not be noticeable.

The Borders

Refer to **Mitered Borders** on page 10 for instructions on how to make and add a mitered border to the quilt top. Sew the red and green border strips together to create the borders. Press the border seam open so that when you add the Template N triangles on top of the border, the border seams will lie flat.

Quilting and Finishing

Make a backing 40" x 40". Layer the backing, batting and quilt top. Quilt as desired. Trim and square the sandwich. Refer to **Binding** on page 12 to make and apply a 3" double-fold binding. Spritz, rinse or wash the quilt to remove any visible water-soluble markings.

Embellishing

Add Swarovski® crystals or other embellishments as desired. For TREASURES, the design in each fabric was used to guide crystal placement.

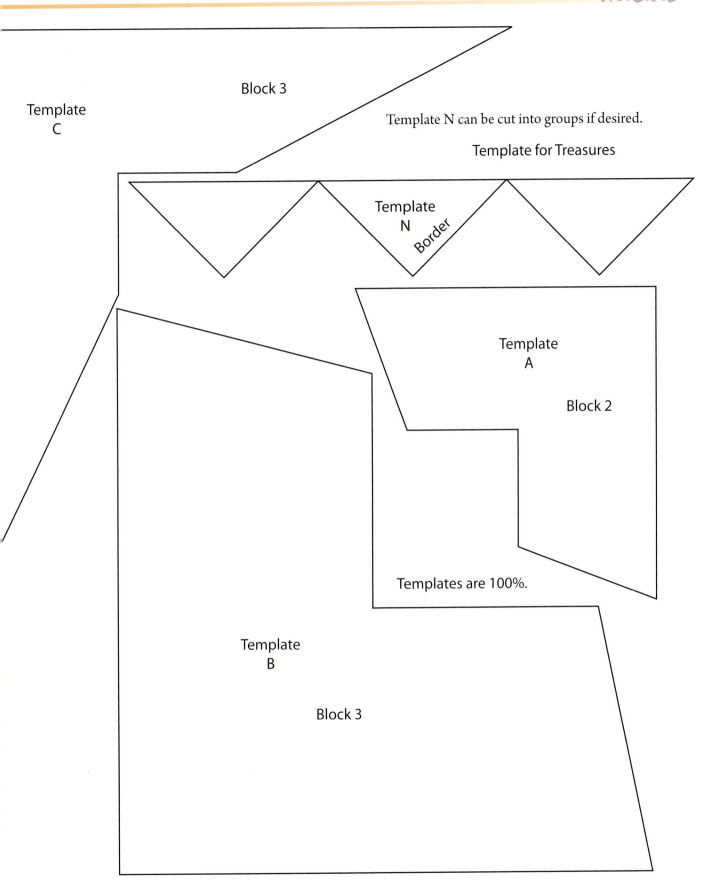

Block 3

Template
C

Template N can be cut into groups if desired.

Template for Treasures

Template
N   Border

Template
A

Block 2

Templates are 100%.

Template
B

Block 3

GALLERY

BASKETS & BLUEBIRDS
44" x 44"
(OUR FAVORITE THINGS)

SUGAR & SPICE
65" x 65"
(BITS & PIECES)

WINK, BLINK AND A NOD
65" x 65"
(SUMMER FUN)

LET IT SNOW
36" x 36"
(MARBLE MANIA)

WOODLAND WEDDING
43" x 43"
(MOTHER'S GIFT)

CORAL TIDES
32" x 32"
(TREASURES)

STACCATO
30" x 30"
(APPLE PICKIN' TIME)

KIMONO PIECES
23" x 23"
(RAPUNZEL'S WINDOW)

PINWHEELS WITH PIZZAZZ
39" x 39"
(SCRAPPY PINWHEELS)

RESOURCES

Sisters blog at
www.quilting-sisters.blogspot.com

Crystals – Cheri's Crystals at
www.cheriscrystals.com or email at
contact @cheriscrystals.com

Fabric – Local quilting stores for the very best fabric available

Threads – Superior® Threads at
www.superiorthreads.com
or email at
info@superiorthreads.com

Tsukineko® ink and dye products – TSC Designs at
http://www.teacherstamp.com

RECOMMENDED READING

The Quilter's Album of Patchwork Blocks & Borders: 4044 Pieced Blocks for Quilters by Jinny Beyer, Breckling Press, 2009.

Machine Appliqué: A Sampler of Techniques by Sue Nickels, American Quilter's Society, 2001.

ABOUT THE AUTHORS

Sisters Ann Seely and Joyce Stewart were raised in Orem, Utah. Ann and her husband, Richard, have three sons and four grandchildren. They live in Taylorsville, Utah. Joyce and her husband, Lynn, have three sons, two daughters, and nineteen grandchildren. They live in Deweyville, Utah.

They began quilting in 1983 and quilting soon became a passion, both separately and together. Ann and Joyce co-authored *Sisters and Quilts: Threads That Bind* (Possibilities, 1992) and *Color Magic for Quilters* (Rodale Press, 1997). They have taught at quilt guilds and quilt shows across the country and have won awards separately and together, including several awards in American Quilter's Society shows.

Joyce   Ann

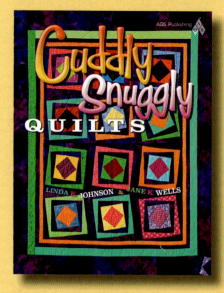
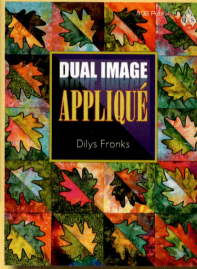
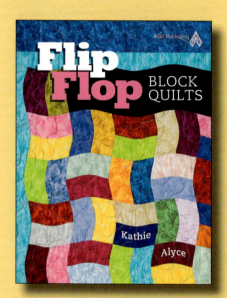
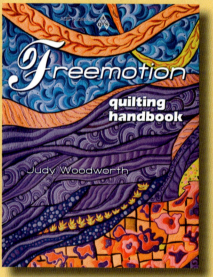
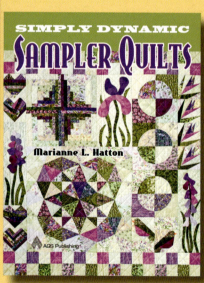
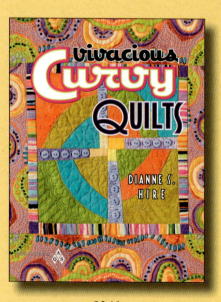